Prais

A Million Miles in a Thousand Years

In his funny, self deprecating style, Donald Miller is sometimes pain-fully honest about his life "unedited," his weaknesses and his faith . . . and that's all I ever choose to read.

— **Tony Hale,**
Actor, *Chuck* and *Arrested
Development*

I love Donald Miller. He is a man after my own heart.

— **Anne Lamott,**
New York Times
best-selling author of
*Traveling Mercies, Grace
(Eventually),* and *Bird by Bird*

If someone tells you they've read this book and they "enjoyed it" or they "liked it" or they think it's a "good book" then maybe they didn't read it—it's well written and funny and interesting and all that, but it's also disturbing. Really, really disturbing. Don is into provocative territory here, wrestling with The Story and the role each our stories play in it . . . this is very convicting, powerful, unsettling writing. I felt like this book read me more than I read it.

— **Rob Bell,**
Author of *Velvet Elvis*

I've never been in Donald Miller's living room, but this book makes me feel that I have. The stories compel, the humor works, and Don's wisdom stealths its way on to the pages. I already want to re-read it.

— **Max Lucado,**
New York Times Best-Selling
Author of *3:16* and *Fearless*

Sly, soulful, and deeply affecting, Donald Miller's *A Million Miles in a Thousand Years* is an indispensable road map and travel companion for readers seeking not only to experience better stories but to live them as well.

— **Allan Heinberg,**
Executive Producer,
Grey's Anatomy

Only Donald Miller can mill the glorious wreckage of the human experience for the hue of jazz and the hope that we can live out a story worth sharing. His premise will haunt you until you set out to discover if memorable lives, like unforgettable books, often require several drafts and a loving editor.

— **Steve Duin,**
The Oregonian

In the first few chapters of Don's new book, Don got me thinking about Don and his interesting life. Then for several chapters, he got me thinking about my own life. And then for the rest of the book, I couldn't help but think about God and other people and the kind of future we're creating together. That sounds like solid evidence that this uniquely talented and sagely writer/thinker/storyteller has given us another wonderful and life-enriching reading experience.

— **Brian McLaren,**
Author, Speaker, Activist,
brianmclaren.net

There are some writers who simply don't have it in them to craft an inelegant sentence. Donald Miller is one of them. *A Million Miles in a Thousand Years* proves in story form how stories define us even more than our genes do. Read this book for an experience of sheer beauty, or for help in living a well-storied life.

— **Leonard Sweet,**
Drew Theological School,
George Fox University,
www.sermons.com

Donald Miller writes, "People love to have lived a great story, but few people like the work it takes to actually live that story." He unpacks what that work looks like and how the story ends! I have great admiration for this storyteller and recommend his latest book with enthusiasm.

— Denny Rydberg,
President, Young Life

This book is an invitation. We're taken on a journey—over mountains and water and across America on a bicycle. We find love and pain along the way, we laugh and we mourn. Through it all, we are invited to live a better story.

— Jamie Tworkowski,
Founder, To Write Love on
Her Arms, www.twloha.com

Donald Miller looks honestly at his own life—and as he examines his own story, he has the courage to take risks and do things that matter. Don is a gifted writer not just because of his winsome and engaging words—but because he encourages us to examine our own lives. From a cross-country bike ride to a living room editing session, Don's scenes invite us to explore our own stories, wherever they may be taking place. I hope you'll take Don up on his challenge and make your own story one worth telling.

— Gary Haugen,
President and CEO,
International Justice Mission;
author, *Just Courage* and
Good News About Injustice

A MILLION MILES IN A

THOUSAND

YEARS

A MILLION MILES IN A

THOUSAND

YEARS

WHAT I LEARNED WHILE EDITING MY LIFE

DONALD
MILLER

THOMAS NELSON
Since 1798

NASHVILLE   DALLAS   MEXICO CITY   RIO DE JANEIRO   BEIJING

© 2009 by Donald Miller

Published in Nashville, Tennessee, by Thomas Nelson. Thomas Nelson is a registered trademark of Thomas Nelson, Inc.

Thomas Nelson, Inc., titles may be purchased in bulk for educational, business, fund-raising, or sales promotional use. For information, please e-mail *SpecialMarkets@ThomasNelson.com.*

ISBN 978-1-4002-0266-9 (IE)

Library of Congress Cataloging-in-Publication Data

Miller, Donald, 1971–
    A million miles in a thousand years : what I learned while editing my life / Donald Miller.
    p. cm.
    ISBN 978-0-7852-1306-2
    1. Miller, Donald, 1971– 2. Christian biography—United States.
3. Autobiography—Authorship. I. Title.
    BR1725.M4465A3 2009
    277.3'083092—dc22
    [B]   2009023464

Printed in the United States of America

09 10 11 12 13 RRD 5 4 3 2 1

Contents

To Kathryn Helmers, for giving me a chance to tell my story.

To Tara Brown, for so kindly organizing my story.

And to Jim Chaffee, for shoving me out the door to tell it.

You have given my narrative depth and joy, and I am so grateful.

Author's Note

IF YOU WATCHED a movie about a guy who wanted a Volvo and worked for years to get it, you wouldn't cry at the end when he drove off the lot, testing the windshield wipers. You wouldn't tell your friends you saw a beautiful movie or go home and put a record on to think about the story you'd seen. The truth is, you wouldn't remember that movie a week later, except you'd feel robbed and want your money back. Nobody cries at the end of a movie about a guy who wants a Volvo.

But we spend years actually living those stories, and expect our lives to feel meaningful. The truth is, if what we choose to do with our lives won't make a story meaningful, it won't make a life meaningful either. Here's what I mean by that:

Part
One

Exposition

one

Random Scenes

THE SADDEST THING about life is you don't remember half of it. You don't even remember half of half of it. Not even a tiny percentage, if you want to know the truth. I have this friend Bob who writes down everything he remembers. If he remembers dropping an ice cream cone on his lap when he was seven, he'll write it down. The last time I talked to Bob, he had written more than five hundred pages of memories. He's the only guy I know who remembers his life. He said he captures memories, because if he forgets them, it's as though they didn't happen; it's as though he hadn't lived the parts he doesn't remember.

I thought about that when he said it, and I tried to remember something. I remembered getting a merit badge in Cub Scouts when I was seven, but that's all I could remember. I got it for helping a neighbor cut down a tree. I'll tell that to God when he asks what I did with my life. I'll tell him I cut down a tree and got a badge for it. He'll most likely want to see the merit badge, but I lost it years ago, so when I'm done with my story, God will probably sit there looking at me, wondering what to talk about next. God and Bob will probably talk for days.

I know I've had more experiences than this, but there's no way I can remember everything. Life isn't memorable enough to remember everything. It's not like there are explosions happening all the time or dogs smoking cigarettes. Life is slower. It's like we're all watching a movie, waiting for something to happen, and every couple months the audience points at the screen and says, "Look, that guy's getting a parking ticket." It's strange the things we remember.

I tried to remember more and made a list, and it pretty much amounted to the times I won at something, the times I lost at something, childhood dental appointments, the first time I saw a girl with her shirt off, and large storms.

● ● ●

After trying to make a list of the things I remembered, I realized my life, for the most part, had been a series of random experiences. When I was in high school, for example, the homecoming queen asked me for a kiss. And that year I scored the winning touchdown in a game of flag football; the guys in the tuba section beat the girls in the clarinet section twenty-one to fourteen. A year or so later I beat my friend Jason in tennis, and he was on the tennis team. I bought a new truck after that. And once at a concert, my date and I snuck backstage to get Harry Connick Jr.'s autograph. He'd just married a Victoria's Secret model, and I swear she looked at my hair for an inappropriate amount of time.

The thing about trying to remember your life is it makes you wonder what any of it means. You get the feeling life means something, but you're not sure what. Life has a peculiar feel when you look back on it that it doesn't have when you're actually living it.

Sometimes I'm tempted to believe life doesn't mean anything at all. I've read philosophers who say meaningful experiences are purely subjective, and I understand why they believe that, because you can't prove life and love and death are anything more than random happenings. But then you start thinking about some of the scenes you've lived, and if you've had a couple of drinks, they have a sentimental quality that gets you believing we are all poems coming out of the mud.

The truth is, life could be about any number of things. Several years ago, my friends Kyle and Fred were visiting Oregon, for instance, and we drove into the desert and climbed Smith Rock. There were forest fires in the Cascade Range that summer, so a haze had settled in the Columbia River Gorge. The smoke came down the river and bulged a deeper gray between the mountains. When the sun went down, the sky lit up like Jesus was coming back. And when the color started happening, my friends and I stopped talking. We sat and watched for the better part of an hour and later said we'd not seen anything better. I wondered then if life weren't about nature, if we were supposed to live in the woods and grow into the forest like tree moss.

But that same year I met a girl named Kim who didn't wear any shoes. She was delightful and pretty, and even during the Oregon winter she walked from her car to the store in bare feet, and through the aisles of the store and in the coffee shops and across the cold, dirty floor at the post office. I liked her very much. One night while looking at her, I wondered if life was about romantic affection, about the thing that gets exchanged between a man and a woman. Whatever I felt for Kim, I noted, I didn't feel for tree moss.

And when my friends Paul and Danielle had their second daughter, I went to the hospital and held her in my arms. She was tiny and warm like a hairless cat, and she was dependent. When I looked over at her mother, Danielle's eyes told me life was about more than sunsets and romance. It was as though having a baby made all the fairy tales come true for her, as though she were a painter who discovered a color all new to the world.

I can imagine what kind of conversation God and Danielle will have, how she'll sit and tell God the favorite parts of the story he gave her. You get a feeling when you look back on life that

that's all God really wants from us, to live inside a body he made and enjoy the story and bond with us through the experience.

Not all the scenes in my life have been pleasant, though, and I'm not sure what God means with the hard things. I haven't had a lot of hard things happen, not like you see on the news; and the hard memories I've had seem like random experiences. When I was nine, for instance, I ran away from home. I ran as far as the field across the street where I hid in the tall grass. My mother turned on the porch light and got in the car and drove to McDonald's and brought back a Happy Meal. When she got home, she held the McDonald's bag high enough I could see it over the weeds. I followed the bag down the walkway to the door, and it shone under the porch light before it went into the house. I lasted another ten minutes. I sat quietly at the table and ate the hamburger while my mother sat on the couch and watched television. Neither of us said anything. I don't know why I remember that scene, but I do. And I remember going to bed feeling like a failure, like a kid who wasn't able to run away from home.

Most of the painful scenes in my life involve being fat. I got fat as a kid and got fatter as an adult. I had a girlfriend out of high school who wanted to see me with my shirt off, but I couldn't do it. I knew if she saw me she would leave. She wouldn't leave right then, but she would leave when she found a nobler reason. She never did, but I never took my shirt off either. I'd kiss down her neck, and she'd reach into my shirt, and I'd pull her hand down, then lose concentration. I suppose a therapist would say this memory points to something, but I don't know what it points to. I don't have a therapist.

When I was in high school, we had to read *The Catcher in the Rye* by J. D. Salinger. I liked the book, but I don't know why. I go back to read it sometimes, but now it annoys me. But I still remember scenes. I remember Holden Caufield in the back of a taxi, asking the driver where the ducks in Central Park go in the winter. And I remember the nuns asking for donations. I remember the last scene in the book, too, when you realize he'd been telling the story to a counselor in a nuthouse. I wonder if that's what we'll do with God when we are through with all this, if he'll show us around heaven, all the light coming in through windows a thousand miles away, all the fields sweeping down to a couple of chairs under a tree, in a field outside the city. And we'll sit and tell him our stories, and he'll smile and tell us what they mean.

I just hope I have something interesting to say.

two

A Million Miles
in a Thousand Years

I STARTED THINKING differently about life when I met a couple of filmmakers who wanted to make a movie about a memoir I'd written. I wrote a memoir several years ago that sold a lot of copies. I got a big head about it for a while and thought I was an amazing writer or something, but I've written books since that haven't sold, so I'm insecure again and things are back to normal.

Before I met the filmmaker guys, I didn't know very much about making movies. You don't think about it when you're watching a movie, but there's a whole world of work involved in making the thing happen. People have to write the story, which can take years; then raise a bunch of money, hire some actors, get a caterer so everybody can eat, rent a million miles of extension cords, and shoot the thing. Then it usually goes straight to DVD. It's a crap job. It made me glad I wrote books.

But I like movies. There's something about a good story that helps me escape. I used to go to movies all the time just to clear my head. If it was a good movie, the experience felt like somebody was resetting a compass in my brain so I could *feel* what was important in life and what wasn't. I'd sit about ten rows back, in the middle, and shovel sugar into my mouth until my brain went numb. And when my brain went numb, I'd get lost in the stories.

I'd go to the movies because for an hour or so I could forget about real life. In a movie, the world faded away and all that mattered was whether the hobbit destroyed the ring or the dog made it home before the circus people could use him as a horse for their abusive monkey.

The movies I like best are the slow literary movies that don't seem to be about anything and yet are about everything at the same time. They are about insecurities and sexual tension and whether the father will stop drinking. I like those movies more because I don't have to suspend as much disbelief. Nobody in real life has to disassemble a bomb, for instance. Not the kind of bomb you think about when you hear the word *bomb*.

• • •

I was sleeping in one morning and got a call from the guy who who had a movie company, and he and his cinematographer wanted to talk to me about an idea. I told him I was planning on seeing a movie that afternoon, the one about the rat that wants to be a chef, and then I wondered out loud how he got my number. "I got your number from your publisher," he said, "and I'm not calling from a theater," he clarified. "I own a movie company. I direct movies."

"That sounds like a good job," I told him, still waking up. "I go to a lot of movies."

"What kind of movies do you like?" the man asked.

"Reese's Peanut Butter Cups," I answered sleepily.

Steve, the movie director, went on to explain he wanted to talk to me about turning my book into a film. He asked again if he could come to town and talk about it. I asked him if he knew where I lived, above the library in Sellwood. He said he didn't, but maybe I could pick him up at the airport.

"Can you repeat what you said about making a movie?" I asked.

"Don, we want to make a movie about your life. About the book you wrote." He said this in a voice that seemed to smile.

"You want to make a movie about *my* life?" I said, sitting up in bed.

"We do. We want to come to town and talk about it. Are you busy the next few days?"

"No," I said. "My roommate is having people over on Sunday, but I wasn't invited."

"We should be gone by Sunday. We were thinking of going out tomorrow."

"Are you going to bring cameras? I need to get a haircut."

"No, we're a long way from that, Don. Can we come out and talk?" he asked.

I realized that I'd heard of Steve before. He used to be in a rock band and when I was a kid I had one of their records. I googled him and he still looked like a rock star. I saw some pictures of him standing behind a camera, wearing a scarf, pointing at somebody to tell them where to stand. His wife was a well known artist, and they'd adopted a child from Africa. He was skinny. I wondered what my life would look like on film. I imagined myself at the theater with a soda in my hand watching myself on the screen doing the things I do in real life. I wondered whether the experience would be like taking a picture of yourself in front of a mirror taking a picture of yourself in front of a mirror.

I wondered whether they wanted to make a documentary about me, because it seems as if life works more like a documentary than a normal movie, and I wondered whether they would show me sitting at my desk smoking a pipe or maybe reading a book while sitting in an oversized chair. I thought maybe my friend Penny could be in the documentary. Maybe Penny and I could be walking through a park, talking. There was a scene like that in my book. I wanted my roommate Jordan to be in it, too, maybe showing him operating the register at the grocery store where he works, or with friends, drafting a fantasy football team this Sunday. I wanted to come, but he said I asked too many questions.

* * *

It snowed the day the filmmakers, Steve and Ben, came to town. And it only snows a few days a year in Portland, so people drive slowly and on the sidewalks thinking it might be safer. People who moved here from Boston come out of the woodwork to tell the natives they don't know how to drive in snow.

I stayed off the highway but still had to navigate the hill on 82nd where the land dips down to the airport. I kept looking around, because everything in the industrial district was cleaner and very heavenly.

Steve and Ben were outside when I rounded the corner and drove under the glass overhang at the airport. Steve, the former rock star, was taller and skinnier than his pictures. He has longish Mick Jagger hair, and though he is fifty or so, he can still get away with designer jeans and shirts with elaborate buttons and bright stitching. Ben, the cinematographer, is about fifty also and had a short-sleeve T-shirt and stood with his hands in his pockets rocking back and forth on his heels to get warm. He looked to be in very good shape, even from a distance, as though he exercises and drinks juices from fruit.

I pulled over a few feet away, but they didn't see me. I watched them for a moment. I wasn't trying to be a spy or anything; it's just that I never know what to say to people when I first meet them. I can get tired when I talk to somebody new, because if there is silence in the conversation, I feel it's my fault. I wondered if I was going to have to spend a couple days with some guys I didn't know and whether there would be awkward silences all the time. I got out of the truck like a real estate agent, though, and introduced myself.

You would have thought I was the king of Persia, because the guys both shook my hand and Ben almost hugged me, and they said they felt like they already knew me after reading my book. They weren't giddy or anything; they were just glad to see me. I don't know how to say it exactly. We put their bags in the back of the truck, and they got in. As I rounded the front of the truck, I stopped, because I noticed snow floating and landing on the enormous glass overhang that covers the front of the airport.

I thought about heaven, about how if we were shooting a movie about heaven, at the airport, we would want to shoot it there, and how in the movie, people would be arriving from earth and from other planets, and when the angels picked us up, they'd put us in their cars and drive a million miles for a thousand years, and it would be miserable until you got to where you were supposed to stay, where you would see your family and the girlfriend you had in the second grade, the girl you always believed was the only one who really loved you.

I got back in the truck and pulled out from under the overhang, and the snow blew softly against the window and melted. The sky was gray-blue, and the weather on the mountains made them look taller. With the city covered in snow, I felt like I was arriving along with my guests. I felt like we were about to explore my same old places in a way that might make them feel new.

---

three

They Fell Like Feathers

WE DIDN'T START talking about the movie right away. We stood on the porch and watched snow make magic of the sky. Steve and Ben live in Nashville, so it doesn't snow that often there either, and we watched it like we were in the second grade. Ben was standing with his eyes toward the sky and letting the snowflakes fall on his face. He had borrowed a jacket, and it fit him too big. He watched the snow as though there were writing on each flake and he was trying to read. He watched each flake as if it were the only one, and they all fell like feathers. He gave us permission to notice how remarkable it was, water frozen and falling from the sky, all the cars stopped and the busses stopped, people out taking pictures of their dogs jumping through snow.

"You have a sled, man?" Ben asked, still reading the snowflakes.

"No. It doesn't snow here much." I wondered whether I'd have a sled if it did.

"We could use trash can lids," Steve said.

"I have two kayaks," I said. I said this because I didn't want them to think I wasn't an outdoorsman just because I didn't have a sled. But I did have kayaks. I got them on clearance at REI the previous year. One night, I and a girl I was dating put in at Oaks Park and paddled into town. The Willamette looks better at night. The lights of the city float on the surface of the river, and you paddle through their reflections like lily-pads. I hadn't used the kayaks since then. We broke up and she moved to Switzerland.

"Kayaks are nice. Kind of a summer thing," Steve said. He was crossing his arms to stay warm.

"Let's have a look at them," Ben said. "Anything will slide, really. Some things slide better than others. But anything will slide." We started walking up the driveway toward the garage. I wondered what we were going to do with the kayaks. My driveway sloped down toward the street, but it wasn't a steep drop. Ben kept looking back at the slope as if it were a river, as though there were rapids flowing over the cement and the ice.

"Did you do a lot of drugs when you were younger, Ben?" I hoped he wasn't offended at the question. He stopped as we walked up the driveway. I turned toward him, and he stood and thought about it for a second. Then he kind of punched me in the chest. "I did, man. I did," he said. "Wow, man, it's like you know me."

• • •

An hour later Ben had tied one end of a rope to a leather steering wheel cover he found in my garage. He'd tied the other end to the back of my truck. I was sitting in a kayak in the middle of the street holding the steering wheel cover. Steve was in the back of my truck, looking at me as though he were going to have to call my mother soon. Ben was in the driver's seat, and Jordan was in the passenger's seat, fidgeting with the stereo.

"I don't know if I want to do this," I whispered.

"Are you saying something?" Steve shouted. Then Ben hit the gas and pulled me through the streets of Sellwood. I went ten blocks then lost control and mounted a curb, lodged the bow of the kayak under a guy's porch, and had to write a small check for a birdbath that honestly didn't fit the dignity of the neighborhood. I kept the pieces, though, because I'd paid for them.

"My turn," Jordan said.

"It steers you left," I warned him.

"It will steer where I tell it to steer," he said in a kind of pretend man voice. I got in the back of the truck with Steve and the birdbath.

"You looked great doing that," Steve said.

"I know," I said.

We watched Jordan for a while, and he figured out how to ride in the ruts. It made me want another turn. But Steve started talking about the movie.

Steve said he liked the book and thought there was a story in it that might make something special onscreen. I couldn't exactly see it, though. The book had been a rambling series of thoughts, mostly essays. I kept seeing a slide show with subtitles. Nobody watches something like that unless James Earl Jones is the narrator. I asked Steve if James Earl Jones was still alive, but he didn't know.

Steve said we might have to create what he called a narrative arc, a structure that would help make sense of the themes for a viewer. At the time I didn't know what he was talking about. He went on to say that in order to turn the book into a movie, we might have to give Don a clearer ambition and put some obstacles in his way. I kept seeing those Japanese game shows where people have to run across padded rolling pins floating over pond water.

He asked if I had a problem with changing things around to create a better story, and I told him I wasn't sure. I used the term *artistic integrity*, which is something I'd heard on National Public Radio.

Steve said he understood how I was feeling, but then his forehead wrinkled like a father about to explain sex. He talked about how books have to be changed for the screen and how people have trouble engaging a story unless the plot is clear. He rattled off the names of several books that had been turned into movies, but I hadn't seen very many of them.

We stopped talking about it for a minute when Jordan ran into a tree. Ben said he wanted to try the kayak. Jordan got in the back of the truck and lay down holding a wadded T-shirt filled with snow up to his nose to stop the bleeding. Steve and I got in the truck.

"Let me put this another way," Steve said. "While you've written a good book, *thoughts* don't translate onto the screen very well. The audience can't get inside your head like they can in a book. They will be restless. They won't engage. Trying to be true to the book is like asking people to read your mind. A story has to move in real life and real time. It's all about action."

"You think they might be bored if we just show my life the way it is," I clarified. I guess I was asking for reassurance that my life was okay.

"I think they'd stab each other in the necks with drinking straws," Steve said. "Nothing against your book. It's a fine book," he added after I'd sat silent for a moment.

I imagined people stabbing each other with straws.

"You in?" Steve asked.

"With their drinking straws?" I asked.

"Crazy, right? We can't let that happen." Steve turned down the radio.

I thought about it for a moment. I thought about artistic integrity. I was going to tell him I needed a couple weeks to consider the idea, but then he said how much he'd pay me, so I told him I'd do it.

---
four

My Real Life Was Boring

STEVE AND BEN left when the snow melted. And I got a contract from Steve a week later. I signed it and sent it back. Then they came again, with sleeping bags and notebook computers. Ben brought me a bottle of wine and handed it to me with a bow around it. Then he drank it that night at dinner. He wanted to go to the store, and I took him, and he looked around for olives. We were walking through Trader Joe's, and he asked what it felt like to edit my life. "What do you mean?" I asked.

"You know. Just to dream it all up again. Everybody wants to go back, man. Everybody wants to make it right. We get to edit your story so it has punch and meaning. That has to be an incredible feeling." I didn't know what to say. I hadn't thought of it like that.

"It's not like it's my real life," I said. "It's just a movie."

"That's true, man," he said, holding a jar of olives. "You can't get your life back." He stood in the aisle, as if he were reflecting. "It's sad, but it's deep." He shook his head as though to grieve something. "What do I know, man? I'm just a cinematographer," he finally said.

"No," I said. "It's true." I was trying to comfort him or something. "We do get to edit a life. It's a fake life, but maybe we will learn something we can apply to our real lives." Ben nearly dropped the olives when I said that. I swear I thought he'd pull out a joint and light it right there in the aisle at Trader Joe's.

"Beautiful, man. We will learn something." He looked at the floor for a second as though to try to remember something, then looked up again. "I got my olives, man," he said. "I just don't think we need anything else from this store. I feel like we got the olives, but we got a whole lot more."

"We should leave, then," I said.

"We should pay for these first," Ben said, holding up the jar.

• • •

"Do you have a whiteboard?" Steve asked. And I did, in the garage. I got it and set it on the mantel.

Ben asked if I had any chips or crackers, and whether I happened to have pipe tobacco. I had all those things and set them on the coffee table, along with a few beers and the olives.

The room held an excitement as though we were drafting for fantasy football.

Steve stood up and began talking. He was tall like a tree; his arms were like thin limbs and his hands were like branches and leaves. He reminded me of David Byrne, the lead singer of the Talking Heads, and I pictured him in a white suit going on about how a particular woman was not his wife. And then he reminded me of Steve Martin, because Steve Martin wore a white suit during his stand-up years. Steve scratched his chest and talked about how it worked to make a movie. He said it can take years, but getting the story right was the foundation. He said he wanted to spend the next several months working on the story.

"We are in for a lot of work," he continued. "But this is the important part, the part nobody sees. The most important element in a movie is the story. It's all about the story." Then Steve turned toward the whiteboard, and it seemed whiter than it had before. His introduction on the importance of story made me think something was going to happen when he stopped talking, but nothing happened. We just looked at the whiteboard. Steve stood with his hands at his sides, as if some magic were going to happen and we were going to come up with *Gone with the Wind* or something.

Ben sat back and put an olive in his mouth and looked up at the board as though he were reading something. He stared so carefully I looked at the board again to see if there was some writing I hadn't noticed. He put the end of his pipe in his mouth and kept looking. I looked at Steve, who was staring at the whiteboard too. I grabbed a few crackers, leaned back, and stared at it myself. I looked at the board so intently I thought I saw a unicorn. Then Steve leaned forward.

"What could we do to get people to like Don?" he asked.

It felt odd hearing my name but having it refer to somebody else who was also me. Ben sat for a second; then he pulled the pipe from his mouth and said Don could work in a factory, a blue-collar job. "Everybody likes the underdog," Ben said. He said this in such a way I wasn't sure if he was talking about *me* or the guy in the movie.

"Are you talking about me?" I asked.

Ben motioned the stem of his pipe toward the empty whiteboard. "The other Don. The fake you," he said, widening his eyes.

"I never worked in a factory," I said, mostly to myself.

"Right, Don," Steve said. "We are going to take the essence of you and *find* the story."

I made a noise as if I understood, but I didn't understand. I know Steve had explained it before but now that we were actually making things up, it felt peculiar. I understood we had to come up with something interesting, but it's not as if we were adapting a novel. Essentially, we were adapting my life. I kept quiet for as long as I could, but when ideas surfaced about me being an expert cat juggler, I had to say something.

"I mean no disrespect," I said. "But what is wrong with the

Don in the book?" The question came out of my mouth more personally than I wanted.

Steve sat thoughtfully and collected his ideas. He scratched his chin and collected some sympathy. "In a pure story," he said like a professor, "there is a purpose in every scene, in every line of dialogue. A move is *going* somewhere."

That last line rang in my ear like an accusation. I felt defensive, as though the scenes in my life weren't going anywhere. I mean, I knew they weren't going anywhere, but it didn't seem okay for anybody else to say it. I didn't say anything; I tried to think about the philosophy of making movies so my face would look like I was thinking something other than the fact that Steve didn't think my life was going anywhere.

"What Steve is trying to say," Ben spoke up, reaching for the jar of olives, "is that your real life is boring."

"Boring?" I blurted.

"Boring," Ben repeated.

"Boring," Steve reluctantly agreed.

I thought about it for a second and then told them about the time I jumped off a bridge, and another time I saw a bear in the woods. "Those times weren't boring," I said.

"Nobody is talking about you, Don." Steve spoke apologetically. "It's kind of true for all of us. Movies don't work like real life. In a story, you arrange life into an understandable series of events so that when the credits roll, people feel satisfied."

"What happened with the bear?" Ben asked.

"He got spooked and ran off," I said.

"Oh," Ben replied, raising his eyebrows as though to confirm that my real life was boring. He pointed the jar of olives at me.

"No thank you," I said.

•　•　•

"We just want to take the basic events of your life and shape them around a structure that makes sense," Steve said, kindly.

I ate a star crunch from the pantry and tried not to look anybody in the eye. "I don't think life works like a formula," I said, perhaps with my mouth full.

"We aren't talking about a formula," Steve said. "We're talking about a few basic principles."

"What's the difference?" I asked.

"Well," Steve said, "it's like music. If I were to play you a recording of a garbage truck backing up, with a jackhammer or something in the distance, that wouldn't be music. That would just be noise, right? I mean you wouldn't exactly get those noises stuck in your head and be humming them a week later."

"Right," I said, wondering if I'd swallowed some of the plastic wrapper around the star crunch.

"But music is different," Steve continued. "Music obeys form and structure. There are scales and harmonics; there are principles a musician adheres to, in order to make music. If he doesn't, it's just noise. It's the same with story. If you don't obey certain principles, the story doesn't make sense. Without story, experiences are just random."

"Experiences are random," I repeated.

"Noise," Ben said.

"Noise," I repeated.

"That's brilliant, right?" I asked Ben.

"Probably," Ben said.

"Are we still talking about the movie?" Steve asked.

"I don't know," Ben said after a moment of silence.

five

Flesh and Soul Better

YOU'D THINK IT wouldn't be a stretch for me to write a movie about my memoir. I'd written the memoir, after all. But I didn't like thinking about myself anymore. You get tired of thinking about yourself all the time when you're a writer. Or at least when you write the kind of books I write. It gets wearisome, all the bellyaching and feeling and thinking about the world and how you interact with it. Everything's a mirror when you're a writer; the computer monitor is a mirror. Who thinks they are so important they need to write books about themselves? Who are these people who write about themselves, and how did I become one of them?

This is how I was thinking when we started writing the movie. I had a deadline on a book, but I stopped answering the publisher's calls. I asked my agent to push the deadline back and got word the publisher was upset. I got word I had a bad reputation, and this scared me. But if I had to write another sentence about myself, about my feelings, I'd vomit.

It was nice to think about the movie, then. And I started thinking about the movie the way Steve and Ben thought about the movie. I thought about the character we were creating as somebody else, somebody who had my name but nothing else in common with me. The guy who was me didn't look like me; he didn't speak like me or act like me. In my head he was better looking; he didn't talk all the time or act silly. He didn't make self-deprecating comments the way I make self-deprecating comments (like a dog that pees when you walk in the room). This Don had some confidence with people, especially women. He was quietly mysterious, dark, and unaffected—the whole bohemian act, but the real of it, the actual thing.

It didn't occur to me at the time, but it's obvious now that in creating the fictional Don, I was creating the person I wanted to be, the person worth telling stories about. It never occurred to me that I could re-create my own story, my real life story, but in an evolution I had moved toward a better me. I was creating someone I could live through, the person I'd be if I redrew the world, a character that was me but flesh and soul other. And flesh and soul better too.

six

My Uncle's Funeral and a Wedding

STEVE AND BEN slept on air mattresses in our living room. I blew up the mattresses and explained that one had a leak. I didn't know which one. "When you feel the floor," I said, "press this button."

There was a fire in the fireplace, and it was flickering against the walls when I turned out the light. Steve looked tall in his pajamas and was shutting down his computer. Ben was in bed already and was taking off his glasses and putting a bookmark in a book.

I went to bed, but I kept the screenplay going in my head. I could hear the conversations the characters were having, and I was steering them into the emotion. I wanted Don to be angry at Penny. I wanted them to fight. I thought the story needed a fight. Steve and Ben said we would have to put Don through a lot of conflict or the story would get boring. I didn't mind putting Don through conflict, because I knew no matter what happened to him we would make things work out before the end.

When Steve, Ben, and I first started working together, I didn't want Don to embrace conflict. I wanted it to be an easy story. But nobody really remembers easy stories. Characters have to face their greatest fears with courage. That's what makes a story good. If you think about the stories you like most, they probably have lots of conflict. There is probably death at stake, inner death or actual death, you know. These polar charges, these happy and sad things in life, are like colors God uses to draw the world.

I was watching the news the other night, and they were still covering that story in Mumbai about the terrorists who went on a shooting rampage. The man on the news said that before the terrorists killed the Jews in the Jewish center, they tortured them. I had to turn off the television, because I could see the torture in my head the way they were describing it. I kept imagining these people, just living their daily lives, and then having them suddenly ended in unjust tragedy. When we watch the news, we grieve all of this, but when we go to the movies, we want more of it. Somehow we realize that great stories are told in conflict, but we are unwilling to embrace the potential greatness of the story we are actually in. We think God is unjust, rather than a master storyteller.

If you want to talk about positive and negative charges in a story, ultimately I think you'd break those charges down into life and death. The fact of life and the reality of death give the human story its dramatic tension. For whatever reason, we don't celebrate coming into life much. I mean we send cards and women have baby showers and all that, but because the baby can't really say thank you, we don't make a big deal out of it. We make a big deal out of death, though. We sit around at funerals, feeling sorry for the unfortunate person whom *death* happened to. We say nice things about the person; we dig a hole and put the body in the hole and cover the casket with all our questions.

I heard that a lot of playwrights used to end their stories with a funeral if it was a tragedy and a wedding if it was a comedy. I think that's why we make such a big deal out of weddings, because a wedding means life, and because the bride and groom are old enough to write a thank-you note for the serving spoons you gave them. And perhaps because you get to drink and dance, no matter how old you are. I only dance at weddings. I practically only drink at weddings, too, mostly because that's where I do my dancing. One of the things that gives me hope is that, even with all the tragedy that happens in the world, the Bible says that when we get to heaven, there will be a wedding and there will be drinking and there will be dancing.

• • •

My uncle Art died this year, and he was a good man. And we didn't have a lot of good men in my family. Not because we had bad ones, but because we didn't have men. My grandfather died when I was a kid, and my dad split about the same time; so did my other uncle. So the only man around the table at Thanksgiving was Uncle Art.

Uncle Art was in his early sixties when he died. My mother called and asked me to pray because he'd had a heart attack. He had just been taken to the hospital, and his heart was barely pumping, and they were going to do surgery. At first I only prayed a little because I found it hard to believe my uncle would die. He was the only man in our family for so long that he was like God. And God doesn't die.

When I was a kid, my uncle had a '57 Chevy truck that ran only half the time. We'd ride in the back of the truck out in back of my grandmother's property. Before my grandfather died, my grandparents had a homestead. It was a piece of land with a creek running through it, and on the other side of the creek there was a track where a man trained horses for racing. That was when my family had some money, when there were men. There was a pasture in front of the house that ran along the street named after my grandfather, then another man's pasture, and in the corner of that man's pasture our family had a piece of land where my great-aunts and uncles were buried, and where my grandfather would be buried when I was too young to remember.

Uncle Art would take us to the cemetery, and I would ride in the back of his truck. We'd spend the day mowing the grass and cutting down limbs. We'd stack the heavy limbs in the middle of the cemetery, and my uncle would douse the pile in gasoline, make a fuse with a line of gas, and let me light the match. You could feel the heat coming off the fire fifty feet away, and the flames punched so high they blew the leaves in the canopy that hung over our dead family. When the fire died down, my uncle would walk to the back of the cemetery and stand at his father's grave with his head down. He'd lean over and wipe off the top of the marker, like an umpire brushing home plate.

That night when my mother called, I stopped working. I closed my laptop and remembered Uncle Art and thought about him standing at his father's grave. I knew he wouldn't die, because his life was like the roots of a tree that went miles into the soil and miles around its trunk and came up in my cousins, in their faces and their voices and their character. I didn't think you could kill a tree that big. Not even God could kill a tree that big.

At the end of his life my uncle ran a boys' camp in Florida and rehabilitated young men the state didn't know what to do with. He spent the day in the sun with these boys, teaching them how to work and how to solve conflicts and get along with each other. I visited him last year, spent a day with the boys in the camp. There was only one building, where the kids ate, and everything else was tents made from logs and tarps. They had built trails connecting the tented areas, and the tents circled around each other and around a stone area that was used as a kitchen. It felt like a village, in the woods in the middle of Florida.

You'd never know the boys were criminals; you really wouldn't. They seemed happy to be there, well behaved. But my uncle said this wasn't the case when they arrived. He said the boys would run away; they didn't trust anybody and were always angry. When I was at the camp, I helped the boys cut wood, and when we were done we jumped in the pond. When there was an argument or one of the boys got out of line, we gathered around my uncle and the boys talked out their differences. My uncle was gentle with them. He'd calm everybody down with his soothing voice, and the boys would confess whatever they had done that was wrong. It was the silliest things, stuff like having a bad attitude or wanting too much attention. But they confessed and they apologized, and my uncle said he wouldn't let the group leave the circle until things were right. They worked like a well-functioning family. My uncle even told me the kids usually didn't want to go home. He said they hated the camp when they arrived, but when it was time to go home, they would cry and beg my uncle to let them stay.

My mom called again and said Uncle Art was gone. She had learned more about what happened. He'd had the heart attack while working out a conflict with the boys in the camp. He collapsed on the ground clutching his chest, and the boy who caused the problem began to cry because he thought it was his fault. He wept and ran into the woods, and later my uncle's own kids had to go looking for him; they had to comfort the boy on the day their father died. My cousin, my uncle's daughter, gave him CPR until the ambulance came. At the hospital his heart beat slowly for a couple of hours and then quit. I still don't know how you could kill a tree that big.

The thing about death is it reminds you the story we are telling has finality. My uncle's funeral was beautiful. I flew down to join the family, and while people were certainly sad, there was also a sense we were burying a good man, which feels different than burying an average man. My uncle's life was celebrated at his funeral. We sang the hymns he loved to sing, and people told stories. His sister, my aunt, stood up and said when my uncle and his family were living in Michigan, he took her out snowshoeing one night. My aunt said the new-fallen snow glowed against the moonlight as though the earth were talking to the sky. At one point, she said, after crossing through some woods, my uncle lifted his hands toward God and recited the verses from the Bible that say, "When I consider thy heavens, the work of thy fingers, the moon and the stars, which thou hast ordained; what is man that thou art mindful of him?"

When we were done at the church, there was a lunch and everyone stayed and ate. I left early to go to the cemetery to make sure the casket was there and ready to be lowered. I had flown in the previous day and hadn't seen the cemetery and had forgotten Hurricane Ike had blown through the previous month. Some distant cousins had come to the cemetery and cleared the trees, the huge limbs that must have fallen in the storm. They'd hauled them off, knowing my uncle's body was coming in from Florida to be buried. I stood in the cemetery by myself, and the grave was in the back, next to my grandfather's. The casket hadn't arrived. The driver was lost, so I stood in the cemetery and gave him directions over the phone. When I hung up, I looked up at the white sky and wished there were a canopy of trees. I remembered the smoke and ash from our fires bellowing up through the canopy, but the canopy was gone.

The man came with the casket, and I helped him unload it from the truck and set it on its stand. The family arrived slowly, car by car, because the road was narrow and there wasn't a place to park. Uncle Art's sister came first and was calm and even smiling. She walked slowly to the casket and when she was within a few feet she lost some strength in her legs and put her arms across the top of the casket and called out for her brother. And then Suzy came into the cemetery with her children, and they sat in the chairs in front of the casket and their friend read from the Bible and told a story about staying up at night to play the banjo with my uncle, and how he loved to sing hymns. And we sang another hymn. Then the men lowered my uncle into the ground.

There were some men standing in the back of the funeral who had dug the grave. One of these men said to me timidly and off to the side that my uncle's funeral was the most meaningful he'd ever seen. He told me he'd seen a lot of funerals, and he wanted me to know that.

My uncle told a good story with his life, but I think there was such a sadness at his funeral because his story wasn't finished. If you aren't telling a good story, nobody thinks you died too soon; they just think you died. But my uncle died too soon.

The next day, when I was walking with my cousin Carol, she asked me where she thought my uncle was. She knew he was in heaven, but she wanted me to tell her what I thought he might be doing, what heaven was like. I told her I thought heaven was outside of time, and perhaps we were already there with her father. She seemed to think that was a nice idea, but I could tell she wasn't comforted. And later that night I pictured Uncle Art, and I could see him in heaven, and he was sitting at a table and there was a celebration. There was dancing and bottles of wine, and there was music. I could see him at a wedding, and I realized that's what I should have told Carol, that her dad was at a wedding.

seven

Going to See the Professor

ON THE FLIGHT home from the funeral, I thought about my uncle's life and wondered what made his life so meaningful. He was like a good movie, in a way, an indie film, perhaps. But a good film, a tear-jerker at the end.

I thought about the elements of our screenplay, then, knowing the elements that made a story meaningful were the same that made a life meaningful.

If Steve was right about a good story being a condensed version of life—that is, if story is just life without the meaningless scenes—I wondered if life could be lived more like a good story in the first place. I wondered whether a person could plan a story for his life and live it intentionally.

I called Steve and asked him how he learned so much about story.

"Are you working on the movie?" he asked, eating a carrot.

"No," I said. "I'm working on *another* project."

"I see," Steve said, still eating his carrot. "Well, I learned about story by taking a class from a guy named Robert McKee."

"You mean like at a community college?" I asked.

"Not exactly. He teaches a seminar called 'Story.' He teaches it a couple of times a year in Los Angeles and New York. The guy knows everything about story," Steve said.

"Do you have his number?" I asked.

"No, Don, it's not like that. But I'll e-mail you the information if you want it."

I told Steve I wanted the information.

Steve said, as a side note, that if I went to the seminar, I should be weary of asking questions, that McKee had little patience with trivial inquiries. He also told me to rent the movie *Adaptation*, because there was a scene in the movie that takes place at one of McKee's seminars. "That will give you a feel for what you're getting into," Steve said.

In *Adaptation*, Nicholas Cage plays a screenwriter with writer's block, so he attends one of Robert McKee's seminars. McKee is played by the actor Brian Cox. He's pacing onstage holding a cup of coffee, a giant movie screen behind him, and he's lecturing with intensity, saying screenwriters should never use voice-over narration, and they shouldn't think their movie could work without an essential structure. And then somebody at the seminar asks a dumb question and McKee slowed to stop. He spoke to the woman in a voice that makes people turn white. He spoke to her until she began to cry, practically. I made a mental note not to ask the real Robert McKee a stupid question, or for that matter, any questions at all.

●   ●   ●

Later, I was eating breakfast with Jordan, who is also a writer, and told him a little about what I was learning. I said I was thinking about attending one of Robert McKee's seminars. Jordan said the best stories have guys with supernatural powers like on that show *Heroes*. He said he was writing a story about a guy who could stop time, like the Japanese character in the television show.

"What's the difference between your character and the guy on *Heroes*?" I asked.

"Ah," Jordan started, pointing a spoon at me. "My character doesn't *know* he can stop time." He looked at me seriously.

So I asked Jordan if he wanted to go to this seminar, thinking the course might help him write his story about the guy who could stop time, and Jordan said yes. In the few weeks before the seminar, I bought McKee's book, a six-hundred-page manifesto on all things story. It read more like a philosophy book, to be honest. Jordan asked why I was reading the book if we were going to go to the seminar, and was there anything in the book about time travel? I told him I was having trouble understanding the book. He said it looked big. He flipped it open and said the type was too small. A few weeks later, we packed our bags and headed to Los Angeles.

"You think Robert McKee will take a look at my story?" Jordan asked.

"Where is your bag?" I responded. Jordan and I were waiting for the shuttle at long-term parking. I had a bag but Jordan didn't.

"Right here," he said, patting his messenger bag.

"Your clothes, I mean. Where are your clothes?"

"I'm wearing them," Jordan said.

"You didn't bring any other clothes?" I asked.

"No. I'm wearing them. These are my clothes." Jordan was wearing shorts, some flip-flops, and a shirt that said ARMY. Jordan used to be in the army. He was pulling a cigarette from behind his ear and was about to light it when the shuttle pulled into the gate. He put it back behind his ear.

"Do you think he will take a look at my story?" Jordan repeated.

"I don't know. Maybe." I pictured Jordan holding out his story in front of Robert McKee and Robert McKee looking at it, dangling there in Jordan's hand, until Jordan finally put it back in his bag.

eight

The Elements
of a Meaningful Life

OUTSIDE THE SEMINAR were slightly overweight writers smoking cigarettes and drinking coffee. They were wearing tweed jackets and scarves—in Los Angeles they were wearing scarves—and were walking around looking at the sidewalk, talking to supposed other people on their cell phones.

I wondered if I were *that kind* of writer, without knowing exactly what I meant by *that kind*. I thought about this while Jordan and I registered, and then I got a cup of coffee and made a couple of calls on my cell phone while Jordan smoked a cigarette. Then we went inside.

We sat on the front row, and Robert McKee came out. He looked like the actor Brian Cox, and he walked like Brian Cox and had his mannerisms, just as Brian Cox had portrayed him in the movie. He had a bottle of water and brought his own glass to pour the water into. He set his notes beside an overhead projector and pulled out slides from his leather briefcase. He walked to the front of the table and put his hands in his pockets and stood straight and smiled. He smiled in a knowing way like he was going to put us through hell and enjoy it, like he was Patton or something.

Robert McKee told us the seminar would be thirty-six hours long. He would lecture for twelve hours each day, and he would take questions during lunch.

"Thirty-six hours?" Jordan leaned toward me and whispered. "*Heroes* comes on at eight o'clock."

He was stark, for sure, and serious, but at the same time didn't seem like a man who would yell. He lectured and was composed and articulate. He had notes, but strayed from them for editorial rants about politics and the Japanese auto industry and old Hollywood. I forgot about the McKee in the movie, the McKee Steve warned me about. This McKee came from another era, when film was supposedly better, when explosions didn't drive the box office, but love did, and tortured souls delivered passionate, overacted monologues in black and white, when fuzzy frames centered on blonde beauties wearing dark, wax lipstick, a single tear rolling down their baby-butt cheeks. There were times during his lectures that I wondered if he were talking to himself. His voice went soft, and he sat on a stool, looking at the floor, and I thought perhaps he was grieving the old stories, wanting them to be told again, or perhaps to have come true. But halfway through the third hour, as though to acknowledge screenwriting had changed, he asked the audience if anybody could give an example of a movie with a good car chase. I wasn't sure if we were supposed to answer his question. Steve said not to ask McKee anything, but could I respond to a question *he* asked? I was curious. And part of me wanted to see if he would get angry like Brian Cox had done in the movie. *A movie with a good car chase?* I told Jordan I'd give him five bucks to yell out *The Passion of the Christ.*

Jordan sat silently for a minute, then he leaned toward me. "I don't think there was a car chase in that movie."

"I'm pretty sure there was," I said.

Then, very suddenly and to my surprise, McKee stood from his chair and pointed his eyes at me. He opened his mouth and spoke softly, softly and yet in a voice that wiped the color from our faces. "This is not grade school, you see!" he said. He spoke in a cadence as though his lines had been practiced in a thousand other lectures having been interrupted by a thousand other morons. He explained in a remarkable economy of words that I was to think of his lecture as theater, not television, and there would be no more commericial breaks in which I could go to the kitchen for ice cream. He kept his eyes pointed at me and after what seemed a perfectly tense moment of silence, he said that if I interrupted him again he would slam my hand in a door. And for a moment, I swear, the room went black and white.

* * *

You'd never know there was so much to learn about story. There are antagonists and protagonists, story turns and transitional dialogue. The whole thing is quite a science, really. Good stories don't happen by accident, I learned. They are planned. And after thirty-six hours of solid lectures in which neither Jordan or I asked a single question, we heard everything there was to hear about story, including what kinds of lightbulbs worked best in the projector that would eventually show our film, and why the Koreans will never make a great sedan.

When he was done, and when the room finished their standing ovation, I sat back in my chair and felt the blood drain from my head. "Thirty-six hours of lectures," I said to Jordan.

Jordan pulled an earphone out of the ear closest to me. "What's that?" he said.

"My mind is fried," I said. "Have you been listening to those things the entire time?"

"Off and on," Jordan admitted, "but that dude is brilliant. Seriously. Who knew?" He nodded his head and put his earphone back in his ear. I pulled a little on his earphone and told him it was over. He closed his laptop and looked around at the empty room. "Brilliant stuff," he repeated.

I went back to the hotel room with two yellow pads full of

notes, an actual script of *Casablanca* that McKee had given us, and the commemorative "Story Seminar" mug, which Jordan had already used as an ashtray.

But even after all those lectures, I wondered what a story actually was. I sat on my bed with my yellow pad and sifted through the pages of notes. I picked up Robert McKee's enormous book and read a few pages before all the words started getting blurry. I set the book down on the bed and looked over at Jordan, who was watching a rerun of *Seinfeld*.

"Positive turn," he said, pointing at the television.

"Jordan," I said.

"What?" he asked.

"After all that, do you understand what a story actually is?" I don't know why I asked. Jordan had taken two pages of notes, one of those pages being the roster for what he called "his players." At the seminar he'd flirted an access code out of a girl at the information center so he could get online. He was online most of the time, adjusting the lineup on his collegiate fantasy basketball team, or e-mailing people on Craigslist asking them whether the poodle they were selling could be trained to fight.

Jordan turned down the volume on the remote and set it against his leg. He looked at me, confused. "That was the point of the seminar, wasn't it?" he asked. "To understand how story worked."

"Right. But it was kind of involved. I don't think I actually picked up the essence of a story."

Jordan looked back at the television and turned up the volume. "A story is a character who wants something and overcomes conflict to get it," he said with remarkable assurance.

"What's that again?" I asked, reaching for a pen and flipping the bulk of pages in my yellow pad over on my lap, arriving at a blank page.

"A character," he said. "Who wants something," he continued. "And overcomes conflict." He paused so I could write it down. "To get it."

I looked at the definition for a second, wondering at how simple it really was. He was right. *A character who wants something and overcomes conflict to get it* is the basic structure of a good story.

"That's it," I said to him. "That's the essence of a story."

"The antagonist!" Jordan shouted, pointing at Newman on the television.

nine

How Jason
Saved His Family

WHEN I GOT back from Los Angeles, I got together with my friend Jason who has a thirteen-year-old daughter. He was feeling down because he and his wife had found pot hidden in their daughter's closet. She was dating a guy, too, a kid who smelled like smoke and only answered questions with single words: "Yeah," "No," "Whatever," and "Why?" And "Why?" was the answer Jason hated most. Have her home by ten, Jason would say. *Why* the guy would ask. Jason figured this guy was the reason his daughter was experimenting with drugs.

"You thinking about grounding her?" I asked. "Not allowing her to date him?"

"We've tried that. But it's gotten worse." Jason shook his head and fidgeted his fingers on the table.

Then I said something that caught his attention. I said his daughter was living a terrible story.

"What do you mean?" he asked.

To be honest, I didn't know exactly what I meant. I probably wouldn't have said it if I hadn't just returned from the McKee seminar. But I told him about the stuff I'd learned, that the elements of a story involve a character who wants something and overcomes conflict to get it. Even as I said this, I wasn't sure how it applied to his daughter.

"Go on," my friend said.

"I don't know, exactly, but she's just not living a very good story. She's caught up in a bad one." I said a lot of other things, and he kept asking questions. We must have talked for an hour or more, just about story, about how novels work and why some movies are meaningful and others simply aren't. I didn't think much of it. I just figured he was curious about movies.

A couple of months later I ran into Jason and asked about his daughter. "She's better," he said to me, smiling. And when I asked why, he told me his family was *living a better story*.

●　　●　　●

The night after we talked, Jason couldn't sleep. He thought about the story his daughter was living and the role she was playing inside that story. He realized he hadn't provided a better role for his daughter. He hadn't mapped out a story for his family. And so his daughter had chosen another story, a story in which she was wanted, even if she was only being used. In the absence of a family story, she'd chosen a story in which there was risk and adventure, rebellion and independence. "She's not a bad girl," my friend said. "She was just choosing the best story available to her."

I pictured his daughter flipping through the channels of life, as it were, stopping on a story that seemed most compelling at the moment, a story that offered her something, anything, because people can't live without a story, without a role to play.

"So how did you get her out of it?" I asked. And I couldn't believe what he told me next.

Jason decided to stop yelling at his daughter and, instead, created a better story to invite her into. He remembered that a story involves a character who wants something and overcomes conflict to get it.

"I started researching some stuff on the Internet," Jason said, "and I came across an organization that builds orphanages around the world. And that sounded to me like a pretty good ambition, something maybe my family could try to do together. It sounded like a good story."

"Right," I said, trying to remember the elements of story myself.

"So I called this organization," Jason continued, "and it takes about twenty-five thousand dollars to build one of these orphanages. And the truth is, we don't have the money. I mean we just took out a second mortgage. But I knew if we were going to tell a good story, it would have to involve risk."

"That's true," I said, remembering it from the seminar.

"So I went home and called a family meeting," my friend continued. "I didn't tell my wife first, which it turns out was a mistake. But I told them about this village and about the orphanage and all these terrible things that could happen if these kids don't get an orphanage. Then I told them I agreed to build it."

"You're kidding me," I said.

"No. I'm not. And my wife sat there looking at me like I'd lost my mind. And my daughter, her eyes were as big as melons and she wasn't happy. She knew this would mean she'd have to give up her allowance and who knows what else. They just sat there in silence. And the longer they sat there, the more I wondered if I'd lost my mind too."

"I actually think you might have lost your mind," I said, feeling somewhat responsible.

"Well, maybe so," Jason said, looking away for a second with a smile. "But it's working out. I mean things are getting pretty good, Don."

Jason went on to explain that his wife and daughter went back to their separate rooms and neither of them talked to him. His wife was rightly upset that he hadn't mentioned anything to her. But that night while they were lying in bed, he

explained the whole story thing, about how they weren't taking risks and weren't helping anybody and how their daughter
was losing interest.

"The next day," he said, "Annie came to me while I was
doing the dishes." He collected his words. "Things had just
been tense for the last year, Don. I haven't told you everything.
But my wife came to me and put her arms around me and
leaned her face into the back of my neck and told me she was
proud of me."

"You're kidding," I said.

"I'm not," my friend said. "Don, I hadn't heard Annie say
anything like that in years. I told her I was sorry I didn't talk to
her about it, that I just got excited. She said she forgave me but
that it didn't matter. She said we had an orphanage to build,
and that we were probably going to make bigger mistakes, but
we would build it." My friend smiled as he remembered his
wife's words.

"And then Rachel came into our bedroom, maybe a few
days later, and asked if we could go to Mexico. Annie and I just
sort of looked at her and didn't know what to say. So then
Rachel crawled between us in the bed like she did when she
was little. She said she could talk about the orphanage on her
web site and maybe people could help. She could post pictures.
She wanted to go to Mexico to meet the kids and take pictures
for her Web site."

"That's incredible," I said.

"You know what else, man?" Jason said. "She broke up with her boyfriend last week. She had his picture on her dresser and took it down and told me he said she was too fat. Can you believe that? What a jerk."

"A jerk," I agreed.

"But that's done now," Jason said, shaking his head. "No girl who plays the role of a hero dates a guy who uses her. She knows who she is. She just forgot for a little while."

Part
Two

A Character

ten

Writing the World

MY FRIEND ANNA works at a soup kitchen, a café downtown run by Catholics. I volunteered there one day, cutting celery, and there was another woman working who had a son who was autistic. Her son sat in a booth and stared at his hands, flicking his fingers in front of his face, watching them like flames.

The boy's mother said he was autistic and sometimes spaced out, staring at his hands, but because I didn't know what autism was, really, I figured he was more or less mesmerized by his existence. I was romanticizing the situation because the kid was probably distracting himself or daydreaming or something, but I thought maybe he was like Hamlet looking at his hands, thinking sincerely about what it means to have been born.

Back when I got out of high school, I used to think about stuff like that all the time. It was a phase, I think, but I used to suddenly realize I was alive and human. I felt like I was in a movie and had two cameras for eyes, and I'd swivel my head around as though I were moving my cameras atop a tripod. I even wrote a poem about it and said we were "spirit bound by flesh, held up by bone and trapped in time." Back then I wondered why nobody else realized what a crazy experience we were all having. Back then I'd be lying in bed or walking down a hallway at college, and the realization I was alive would startle me, as though it had come up from behind and slammed two books together. We get robbed of the glory of life because we aren't capable of remembering how we got here. When you are born, you wake slowly to everything. Your brain doesn't stop growing until you turn twenty-six, so from birth to twenty-six, God is slowly turning the lights on, and you're groggy and pointing at things saying *circle* and *blue* and *car* and then *sex* and *job* and *health care*. The experience is so slow you could easily come to believe life isn't that big of a deal, that life isn't staggering. What I'm saying is I think life is staggering and we're just used to it. We all are like spoiled children no longer impressed with the gifts we're given—it's just another sunset, just another rainstorm moving in over the mountain, just another child being born, just another funeral.

I had a friend who ate a certain kind of mushroom, and

said she got in touch with the staggering nature of life for a couple of hours. She sat on her haunches and looked over a blade of grass and realized all the organisms living on the blade were like tiny humans living in a tiny skyscraper of grass, and to them she was like a monster. It sounded interesting until an ant crawled to the top of the blade of grass, raised its fist, and challenged her for being a socialist. Then a tree bent down and hung her from her ankles for the rest of the night.

When Steve, Ben, and I wrote our characters into the screenplay, I felt the way I hope God feels as he writes the world, sitting over the planets and placing tiny people in tiny wombs. If I have a hope, it's that God sat over the dark nothing and wrote you and me, specifically, into the story, and put us in with the sunset and the rainstorm as though to say, *Enjoy your place in my story. The beauty of it means you matter, and you can create within it even as I have created you.*

I've wondered, though, if one of the reasons we fail to acknowledge the brilliance of life is because we don't want the responsibility inherent in the acknowledgment. We don't want to be characters in a story because characters have to move and breathe and face conflict with courage. And if life isn't remarkable, then we don't have to do any of that; we can be unwilling victims rather than grateful participants.

But I've noticed something. I've never walked out of a meaningless movie thinking *all* movies are meaningless. I only thought the movie I walked out on was meaningless. I wonder, then, if when people say life is meaningless, what they really mean is *their* lives are meaningless. I wonder if they've chosen to believe their whole existence is unremarkable, and are projecting their dreary life on the rest of us.

---

eleven

Imperfect Is Perfect

WE WERE WRITING AGAIN. Steve decided to make the film, so we set up weeklong writing sessions in which they would come to Portland or I would meet them in Nashville. We were back in Portland and I was excited. I knew all about story at this point, about how you have to create a character who wants something and overcomes conflict to get it. I was ready to win an Academy Award and everything. I had my speech written, the dramatic pause and grand gestures, the whole "I never thought this would happen to me" bit. They came at night and we talked till late but didn't work. I wanted to work, but the conversation never turned to the movie. They said we'd tackle it in the morning. So I was the first to wake, and from the kitchen I could see Steve and Ben under their blankets in the living room. I put coffee on, thinking the smell of coffee might get them going. And when it didn't, I rattled pans until their blankets moved. Steve got up and came into the kitchen on the way to the bathroom, and I asked him if he wanted eggs.

He squinted at me and rubbed his chin and looked down at the frying pan. "Eggs," he said before turning toward the bathroom.

"What kind of eggs?" Ben said loudly from under his covers.

"Chicken ones," I said.

"My favorite," he replied.

I made three plates of eggs and sat on the couch and stared at the whiteboard. We'd decided our character lived in Texas, like I did when I was his age, and his mom was single, and he worked in a factory but wanted to escape his small town. That's all we had from our previous session. Ben sat next to me still in his pajamas and shook pepper on his eggs. He looked at the whiteboard and made a humming noise. I made a humming noise too.

"What happens next?" I asked.

"An explosion," Steve said, coming back into the room with his plate.

"Really?" I asked.

Steve shrugged his shoulders as though to say, "Why not?" Then Ben chewed and talked and reminded us we were on a budget.

"What do we *want* to happen?" Steve asked.

"We want Don to beat somebody up or something," I said. "And get a lot of money and a new car."

"Or we could just find the money for that explosion," Ben said, sliding his fork under a plume of egg.

•   •   •

We were all eating, which was nice, because it distracted us from the silence. I'd imagined the morning differently, us talking over each other and scrambling to write on the whiteboard, high-fiving each other and saying, "Yeah, yeah, that's it, and then he can kiss her!" But the whiteboard sat quietly on the mantel looking at us disappointedly, watching us move our eggs around. The scraping of our plates and the slurping of our coffee got loud, and the longer we went without talking, the more I felt our story dying. Finally, Ben said something.

"Where is Don's father?"

•   •   •

I didn't know what Don's father had to do with anything. We'd just been talking about what Don wants. We needed Don to want something.

My reaction was nearly physical. I put my plate down and crossed my legs and was suddenly aware of what my hands were doing and where my eyes were looking.

In my memoir, I'd talked about my father, and how basically

I didn't have one. Ben brought that up. He said he thought the father should be in the story and we should show how Don longs for that relationship. In the movie, Ben wanted Don to sit on the edge of his bed and look at a picture of his dad.

Absurd. *I never sat on my bed and looked at a picture of my father,* I thought to myself. *I never even knew my father.*

"It's cliché," I said.

"No," Steve disagreed. "I don't think its cliché. That's a situation a lot of people can identify with."

"We're not making a movie about a college kid who misses his dad," I said.

"That's not what it's about," Steve said. "But it fleshes Don out. It makes him real. Characters need to be real, to be human."

I shrugged my shoulders.

"What if he lost his dog?" I offered. "We could give him a dog and the dog could run away." Steve and Ben didn't high-five me. They didn't say. *Yeah, yeah. And then he could kiss the girl.*

"We're trying to figure out the conflict of the story," Steve said. "It has to be real conflict. If the story is going to be good, Don is going to have to face some stuff he doesn't want to face."

I wondered whether Steve was talking about me or the yahoo we were writing a screenplay about. I was trying not to think about what my hands were doing. They were on my knees, but that didn't feel natural. Both Steve and Ben were looking at me through the corners of their eyes, and I was looking at them through the corners of my eyes too. I was getting a headache from looking where I wasn't looking.

•   •   •

I hadn't seen or talked to my dad in more than thirty years. He disappeared when I was a kid, and Mom never talked about him. It was as if he didn't exist. Sure, I wondered every once in a while where he was. I knew they were married, because my mom was divorced. And I knew he was a basketball coach, because I have memories of being with him in the gym during practice. But I'd avoided him ever since I could. I didn't long for him. In fact—and I didn't know this while we were writing—I was afraid he'd rejected me for a reason, that he somehow knew I'd grown up and become fat. At the time we started writing the movie, I was still pretty fat. I was afraid my father would reject me because I wasn't an athlete. And I was deathly afraid of finding out that was true.

"This endears us to Don, man," Ben said, breaking the silence. "We still don't know what he wants, but the father subplot will make him human. He's vulnerable you know?"

He's a loser, I thought.

"Maybe he can also be in love with a girl who doesn't love him back?" Steve suggested.

This isn't happening, I thought. I wanted to go back to bed.

•   •   •

But I kept thinking about the stuff we learned in the Robert McKee seminar. I knew from Jason's story that the same elements that make a movie meaningful are the ones that make a life meaningful. I knew a character had to face his greatest fears. That's the stuff of good story.

I also knew from the McKee seminar that most of our greatest fears are relational. It's all that stuff about forgiveness and risking rejection and learning to love. We think stories are about getting money and security, but the truth is, it all comes down to relationships. I tried not to think about that stuff, but I couldn't get it out of my mind. I knew a story was calling me. I knew I was going to have to see if my father was alive. And once you know what it takes to live a better story, you don't have a choice. Not living a better story would be like deciding to die, deciding to walk around numb until you die, and it's not natural to want to die.

•   •   •

We plotted a few more scenes, and then late that morning Ben and I took a break and smoked our pipes on the balcony. Whenever Ben and I took a smoke break, Steve would stay inside and type whatever was on the whiteboard into his computer.

"We got some stuff down," I said to Ben, acknowledging I was at least considering the father subplot perhaps.

"Yeah, man," Ben said. "I feel good about it." Ben blew smoke up and around him and brushed his hair back from his eyes. I was surprised at how much emotion I was feeling. It wasn't sentimental or sad, just that same fear I was telling you about.

"You know, man. It's going to be a beautiful story," Ben said, as though he could see the worry on my face.

"You think?" I asked.

"I think," he said.

"Where do you think the story is going?" I asked Ben.

"Who knows, man?" Ben said, grinning. "That's why we're interested, right?"

"Right," I said, as though it were a matter of fact. "And what exactly are we interested in?"

"You know, man," Ben said, still smiling. He took a drag from his pipe and spoke as he blew out the smoke. "Is Don going to get his life together or not?" He looked at me as though he wanted me to respond. He kept looking at me, the smoke billowing around his eyes.

"I don't know," I finally answered. Ben nodded his head and grinned, taking another drag on his pipe.

"Oh, he will," Ben said. "He certainly will."

twelve

You'll Be Different at the End

IF THE POINT of life is the same as the point of a story, the point of life is character transformation.

If I got any comfort as I set out on my first story, it was that in nearly every story, the protagonist is transformed. He's a jerk at the beginning and nice at the end, or a coward at the beginning and brave at the end. If the character doesn't change, the story hasn't happened yet. And if story is derived from real life, if story is just a condensed version of life, then life itself may be designed to change us, so that we evolve from one kind of person to another.

I have a friend named Marcos who was an art student at Reed College in Portland. For his senior thesis, he studied human beings as they physically mature. He used his own body for part of the story, carefully weighing each limb, inspecting his hands under a microscope, and photographing himself with varying facial hair configurations. It was a strange thesis, even for an art student, and especially considering he devoted nearly a year of his life to the work. But what Marcos was trying to figure out was worth it; he was trying to understand whether our physical bodies said something about our philosophical reality.

When he finished, I asked Marcos what he'd discovered; and he said, essentially, humans are alive for the purpose of journey, a kind of three-act structure. They are born and spend several years discovering themselves and the world, then plod through a long middle in which they are compelled to search for a mate and reproduce and also create stability out of natural instability, and then they find themselves at an ending that seems to be designed for reflection. At the end, their bodies are slower, they are not as easily distracted, they do less work, and they think and feel about a life lived rather than look forward to a life getting started. He didn't know what the point of the journey was, but he did believe we were designed to search for and find something. And he wondered out loud if the point wasn't the search but the transformation the search creates.

And that seemed fascinating to me.

"What do you mean?" I asked.

Marcos explained that our bodies were designed to change,

and it isn't possible to be stagnant. He showed me a slide of himself at the beginning of the year and of the new lines on his face that had deepened since. He said our interaction with each other, with the outside world, and with intangible elements such as time made us different people every season. His conclusion was that the human body displayed physical evidence that we are not the same person we were when we were kids, or even a season before. He said we think we are the same person, but we aren't. "People get stuck, thinking they are one kind of person, but they aren't."

For instance, Marcos said, "The human body essentially recreates itself every six months. Nearly every cell of hair and skin and bone dies and another is directed to its former place. You are not who you were in February," he told me.

I thought about Marcos's conclusions and wondered how much his education cost his parents. But I also wondered if he wasn't right, that we were designed to live through something rather than to attain something, and the thing we were meant to live through was designed to change us. The point of a story is the character arc, the change.

thirteen

A Character Is What He Does

ONCE I UNDERSTOOD the power of story in my personal life, I wanted to know more about how to create a good one. I was getting up a little earlier, and interestingly enough, I was going to fewer movies. In a way, I'd started a new story about trying to find a story, and so I didn't need to escape my boring life anymore. I was a character who wanted something, and, well, that's half the battle. And I kept learning more about story. I learned that not just any character can work to create a good story. It takes a specific kind of character. And not just any ambition would define a good story. It took a specific kind of ambition. The elements of story were conditional, in other words. These conditions were fixed principles too, and every good screenwriter knows them the way a musician knows his scales.

. . .

"I think Don is really angry at this point," I said.

Steve, Ben, and I were talking about a critical scene at the end of Act I of our screenplay, a scene that launches our character into the story. "I think he's angry and he's had enough," I said.

Steve nodded in agreement. "But how do we show his anger on the screen? How do we tell the audience he's angry?" he asked.

"We just say it," I said.

"We can't say it, Don. It's not a book; it's a movie. We have to show it. A character is what he does."

. . .

A couple of weeks later, I ran into a friend I hadn't seen in years. We had some time, so we walked down to the Ugly Mug for coffee. I caught him up on stuff in my life then asked what was going on in his. He said he and his wife had a baby since he last saw me. A little girl. He pulled out his wallet and showed me pictures. I asked him if it was scary being a father, and he told me, no, he loved it. He said his life had gotten smaller. His world had shrunk to his wife and his kid, and all that mattered was keeping them safe.

"Your wife must be loving you," I said.

My friend went on to say he was more in love with his

wife than ever, which is not something men usually say to each other, even if it's true. I don't know why we don't say those things, but we don't. So I knew he must really be crazy about his wife. He said he'd been preoccupied with work and hadn't paid much attention to life at home; but after the baby came, he saw his wife differently.

"She's amazing," my friend said, shaking his head. "A baby came out of her body, for crying out loud. And now she produces food. She keeps the baby alive."

I asked him how his wife felt about all of this, thinking she must be excited to have her husband back. My friend looked at me as though he were realizing he hadn't actually said anything to his wife.

"You haven't said anything?" I questioned.

"I guess I figured she knew," my friend suggested.

And that's the first time I realized that the idea *a character is what he does* makes as much sense in life as it does in the movies. I thought about my friend's story from his wife's perspective. She only knows what he says and what he does, not what he thinks and what he feels. I'm sure his wife picked up on his newfound enthusiasm, but it did help me realize the stories we tell ourselves are very different from the stories we tell the world. I told him he ought to bring her flowers. He said that was a good idea and asked me where he could get flowers.

Robert McKee talks about character revelation in his book: "Beneath the surface of characterization," he says, "regardless of appearances, who is this person? At the heart of his humanity, what will we find? Is he loving or cruel? Generous or selfish? Strong or weak? Truthful or a liar? Courageous or cowardly? The only way to know the truth is to witness him make choices under pressure, to take one action or another in the pursuit of his desire."

Of all the principles I'd learn about story while working with Steve and Ben, the idea that a character is what he does remains the hardest to actually live.

I live in fantasies. I live terrific lives in my head. It's part of the creative imagination, to daydream, to invent stories.

When I was young, I used to watch this cartoon about a kid who got lost in daydreams. He'd zone out during class and imagine himself in the jungle fighting toothy animals. In the cartoon he'd be shaken by the jaws of a lion, right about to die, and come out of his daydream with his teacher standing above him, shaking him awake.

I think I grew up to become that kid. As a writer, I've turned daydreaming into a cottage industry. I make stuff up and sell it. I realized this was true recently while writing at a friend's cabin on Orcas Island. I'd gone there because there's nothing to do on the island but write. I can't write at home because there are too many phone calls and e-mails and it's harder to work.

But even on the island, when I should have been writing, I'd take long walks along the water and imagine myself having been a captain lost at sea. It's embarrassing to admit this, but it's true. In my mind I could see a boat washing up on the shore and I imagined myself climbing out of it with a long beard, smoking a pipe, being greeted by local villagers who were hungry for stories about life on the ocean.

I didn't know getting lost in daydreams was odd until a couple of years ago when I asked an old girlfriend what she daydreamed about. She answered, "Nothing." *How does a person daydream about nothing?* I wondered. But she explained she lived in the now and worked with whatever was really happening.

In the room where I'm writing today, nothing is happening. And later there will be laundry happening, which is nothing to daydream about. I can't deal with reality.

But last year I was sitting in a café in Boston when a man came in with his wife and their two children. One of the children was a boy who looked to be three, and the other was an infant dressed in pink. I went back to reading, but after a time the infant began to cry in a shrill I would normally find annoying. But it didn't affect me the same way this time. I watched the mother lift the baby into her lap and comfort her until the child's sobbing turned to gasping. As the mother brought the child to her shoulder and rocked her until gasping turned back to breathing. It hit me then that while I had spent my twenties daydreaming and avoiding the reality of crying children, this man I didn't know had met a woman and started a real family with real children who were not literary inventions, but actual characters who cried in coffee shops. This sort of life once sounded boring to me. It was too real, too unromantic, I suppose. But there in Boston it occurred to me that his story was better than mine for the simple fact that his story was actually happening. He was doing real things with real people while I'd been typing words into a computer.

When I arrived home from Boston, I realized there were no pictures on my mantel. I set down my suitcase and walked into the living room and looked across to the fireplace, and it felt empty. Empty of real stories. I went into my bedroom where the bed was made, and on my desk there were no pictures in frames and on the end tables there were no pictures. There was a framed picture of Yankee Stadium above the toilet in the bathroom, and there was some art I'd picked up in my travels, but there was little evidence of an actual character living an actual life. My home felt like a stage on which props had been set for a fake story rather than a place where a person lived an actual human narrative.

It's an odd feeling to be awakened from a life of fantasy. You stand there looking at a bare mantel and the house gets an eerie feel, as though it were haunted by a kind of nothingness, an absence of something that could have been, an absence of people who could have been living there, interacting with me, forcing me out of my daydreams. I stood for a while and heard the voices of children who didn't exist and felt the tender touch of a wife who wanted me to listen to her. I felt, at once, the absent glory of a life that could have been.

• • •

I was watching a reality show on television about this time, and I wondered what a show might look like if a camera followed me around. I wondered what people would think. That is, setting aside my daydreams and wants and thoughts and revealing my life through an objective camera lens. The thought was humbling. In truth, I was a person who daydreamed and then wrote down his daydreams. Sure, there were other characters, friends and business associates, but I wasn't living any kind of sacrifice. My entire life had been designed to make myself more comfortable, to insulate myself from the interruption of my daydreams.

• • •

I thought again about my father, about how a story was calling to me. I worried again that he might be dead, or worse, alive. But I knew I needed to *do* something. I needed to live a real story with real action.

Later, Steve, Ben, and I were back in Nashville at our friend Jim's house, and we were standing out on the back deck. We were writing that scene where Don sits on the edge of his bed and looks at a picture of his father. Ben was lighting up his pipe and was looking reflective.

"It's powerful stuff," he said. "People don't talk about it, but it's powerful stuff, man."

"The father stuff?" I said.

"Right, man."

"Do you know your dad?" I asked.

"No. My Dad was like twenty years older than my mom." I looked at him surprised. "Yeah, man." He continued, "He bagged a trophy. And, well"—Ben held out his arms and smiled—"here I am, man. They made me."

"That's crazy. We should be writing a movie about you," I said.

"Oh yeah. That would be a story for sure. But no, I never really knew him. He died when I was a kid. I never really thought about him. Same as you, I guess," Ben said, knowing part of my story.

"Some stories don't really have closure, I guess," I said.

"Oh man, no. Mine does. After I got married, my wife, Elaine, and I went back to San Francisco, you know. We found the cemetery where he was buried. I didn't think much of it because we weren't in San Francisco to see my father's grave. It was just a wild hare. Elaine was saying we should do it; she was saying we should go visit his grave. I gave the guy at the cemetery my father's name, and we found the grave up on the side of a hill there, a great spot. Elaine stood back, and I walked up to the grave, and man, I just started weeping. I wasn't expecting to feel anything, but it's powerful. You don't know it's there, but it's there. Something is there. So I said good-bye to him. Well, I guess I said hello to him and introduced myself, and then

I said good-bye to him. Elaine came over, and I introduced her to him, and I introduced the guy who worked at the cemetery too, but I imagine they'd met before. It was powerful, man."

"That is powerful," I said.

fourteen

Saving the Cat

I DON'T KNOW why we need stories, but we always have. I'd say it's just that we like them, that they're entertaining, but it's more than that. It's a thing in us that empties like a stomach and then needs to be filled again.

This is how it has always been. The ancients who painted hieroglyphics, the orators telling the news, the children in their beds while their parents made up heroes and dragons, and then the three of us, sitting in the living room with scraps of paper all over the floor and on the coffee table, with two whiteboards filled from one side to the other with ink, with time lines, with this happens and then this happens and then another thing.

I hadn't loved the process of writing so much in years. Steve and Ben were sitting, but I paced, and I only pace when

I'm engaged. Some people say a writer catches spirits, and the spirits whisper lines inside his brain. It feels like this at times. It feels like there are spirits. I paced and I was catching spirits. I said I thought Don should try to sleep with Penny. We were trying to create tension between the Don character and the Penny character, and I thought he should make a move on her, just press against her in the hallway when they went back to her dorm room. I wanted him to put his hands on her sides and try to kiss her neck. She could resist, but he would still put his head down to her neck.

"It's too early for that," Steve said. "Don can't make a move on Penny, not in the way you're describing."

"Why not?" I asked.

"It's too early," Steve repeated, and Ben agreed.

"But we need the tension," I countered.

Ben asked if I'd read a book called *Save the Cat*. I told him I hadn't. He said it was a screenwriters' book, a how-to for writing movies. I didn't know what that had to do with Don making a move on Penny, but Ben explained *Save the Cat* comes from a trick storytellers use to engage an audience. In the first twenty minutes of the story, Ben said, your protagonist has to do something good. He can be crabby and have a drinking problem and even be a bit of a jerk, but unless he does something good, the audience won't want things to work out for him, and they'll lose interest in your story. "We have to see that Don has a good heart," Ben said. "He has to save a cat."

"Did you see the new *Rocky* movie?" Steve asked.

I had.

Steve put his yellow pad on the table. He asked what I remembered about the movie, and I told him I remembered Rocky fought a kid who was the heavyweight champion, and Rocky was trying to reunite with his son. And I remembered that he went all twelve rounds and ended up winning, basically, just like every other *Rocky* movie.

"Anything else you remember?" Steve asked.

"Not really," I said.

So Steve walked me through the first thirty minutes of the film, and I was surprised at all the stuff I didn't remember. He said in the first thirty minutes of the movie, Rocky grieves his wife, actually going out in the streets and crying; and he gives food to a homeless man who comes by the small restaurant he owns; and he stands at people's tables at the restaurant and tells stories about his years as the champ, because many of his guests want him to tell stories. He tells story after story as though it is the first time he is telling them, even though he has to tell the stories every night. Then he befriends a single mom, gives her a job, and doesn't even try to sleep with her. He takes her home one night and pulls a lightbulb out of his pocket and screws the bulb into the socket on the porch, saying she shouldn't be walking around in that neighborhood in the dark. Then he starts befriending the single mom's kid, a teenager about to screw up his life. And if that weren't enough, if that didn't make Rocky the Mother Teresa of boxers, the teenager and Rocky go to a dog shelter and adopt the ugliest dog you could imagine. "Do you remember any of that?" Steve asked.

"Some of it," I said. "Now that you mention it."

"The thing is," Steve continued, "it was a movie about boxing. But the first half hour was this charity stuff, right?"

"Right," I said.

"If he didn't do all those things," Steve said, "we wouldn't care whether he went twelve rounds or not. We'd have gotten to the end of the movie and not cared a bit. We wouldn't know why we didn't care; we'd just say it wasn't a very good movie. But the reason would have been that the guy who won in the end wasn't really a good guy. He was just a normal guy."

fifteen

Listen to Your Writer

A WHILE BACK I was working on a novel about a performance artist-turned-ecoterrorist. I never published it because, well, it was about a performance artist-turned-ecoterrorist, and I couldn't exactly find a market for the story. But I was writing a novel all the same, and I was doing it in an office on the other side of the tracks. I wasn't living where I live now; I was living in Eastmoreland, the neighborhood with the old trees and the houses that look like English bungalows with rose gardens flowering over their fences and gates.

I'd get up in the morning and make coffee and toast, I'd put my laptop in a backpack and put on a raincoat, and then I'd walk from my house through the neighborhood, through all those gardens, to the office on the other side of the tracks.

I'd create my stories while I walked, thinking about what I wanted my characters to do, what I wanted them to say, and how I wanted them to throw headlong into whatever scene was coming next. I felt like God when I walked, always making worlds, and I believed when I arrived at my building and climbed the stairs and went into my office and shut the door, I would sit down and bring these worlds to life. But this never happened.

It was a half-hour walk, so by the time I got to my desk, I'd had plenty of time to plan whatever was coming in the book. But stories are only partly told by writers. They are also told by the characters themselves. Any writer will tell you characters do what they want.

If I wanted my character to advance the plot by confronting another character, the character wouldn't necessarily obey me. I'd put my fingers on the keyboard, but my character, who was supposed to go to Kansas, would end up in Mexico, sitting on a beach drinking a margarita. I'd delete whatever dumb thing the character did and start over, only to have him grab the pen again and start talking nonsense to some girl in a bikini. He'd do this, remember, in a story about a performance artist-turned-ecoterrorist.

And as I worked on the novel, as my character did what he wanted and ruined my story, it reminded me of life in certain ways. I mean as I sat there in my office feeling like God making my worlds, and as my characters fought to have their way, their senseless, selfish way of nonstory, I could identify with them. I fought with my ecoterrorist who wanted the boring life of self-indulgence, and yet I was also that character, fighting God and I could see God sitting at his computer, staring blankly at his screen as I asked him to write in some money and some sex and some comfort.

I like the part of the Bible that talks about God speaking the world into existence, as though everything we see and feel were sentences from his mouth, all the wet of the world his spit.

I feel written. My skin feels written, and my desires feel written. My sexuality was a word spoken by God, that I would be male, and I would have brown hair and brown eyes and come from a womb. It feels literary, doesn't it, as if we are characters in books.

You can call it God or a conscience, or you can dismiss it as that intuitive knowing we all have as human beings, as living storytellers; but there is a knowing I feel that guides me toward better stories, toward being a better character. I believe there is a writer outside ourselves, plotting a better story for us, inter-acting with us, even, and whispering a better story into our consciousness.

As a kid, the only sense I got from God was guilt, some-thing I dismissed as a hypersensitive conscience I got from being raised in a church with a controlling pastor. But that isn't the voice I'm talking about. That voice really *was* the leftover hypersensitive conscience I got from being raised in a church with a controlling pastor.

The real Voice is stiller and smaller and seems to know, without confusion, the difference between right and wrong and the subtle delineation between the beautiful and profane. It's not an agitated Voice, but ever patient as though it approves a million false starts. The Voice I am talking about is a deep water of calming wisdom that says, *Hold your tongue; don't talk about that person that way; forgive the friend you haven't talked to; don't look at that woman as a possession; I want to show you the sunset; look and see how short life is and how your troubles are not worth worrying about; buy that bottle of wine and call your friend and see if he can get together, because, remember, he was supposed to have that conversation with his daughter, and you should ask him about it.*

So as I was writing my novel, and as my characters did what he wanted, I became more and more aware that somebody was writing me. So I started listening to the Voice, or rather, I started calling it the Voice and admitting there was a Writer. I admitted something other than me was showing a better way. And when I did this, I realized the Voice, the Writer who was not me, was trying to make a better story, a more meaningful series of experiences I could live through.

At first, even though I could feel God writing something different, I'd play the scene the way I wanted. This never worked. It would always have been better to obey the Writer, the one who knows the better story. I'd talk poorly about somebody and immediately know I'd done it because I was insecure, and I'd know I was a weak character who was jealous and undisciplined.

So I started obeying a little. I'd feel God wanting me to hold my tongue, and I would. It didn't feel natural at first; it felt fake, like I was being a character somebody else wanted me to be and not who I actually was; but if I held my tongue, the scene would play better, and I always felt better when it was done. I started feeling like a better character, and when you are a better character, your story gets better too.

At first the feeling was only about holding my tongue. And when I learned to hold my tongue a bit, the Voice guided me from the defensive to the intentional. God wanted me to do things, to help people, to volunteer or write a letter or talk to my neighbor. Sometimes I'd do the thing God wanted, and the story always went well, of course; and sometimes I'd ignore it and watch television. But by this time I really came to believe the Voice was God, and God was trying to write a better story. And besides, nothing God wanted me to do was difficult.

Until. . . .

I was driving over the Bybee Bridge and listening to *Talk of the Nation* on NPR when a story came on about a man who was reunited with his father whom he hadn't seen in twenty years. I listened to the story apathetically, not applying it to my life, when suddenly the Voice, and I am talking about the Writer who is not me, pounded on the keyboard, broke the pencil on the paper, and was so emphatic that I had to pull my truck over by the golf course. After thirty years of, honestly, never thinking about it or having anything like a desire to do so, the Writer who is not me told me I was to find my father.

I told the Writer no. I sat in my car by the golf course and told the Writer no. I know he had talked to me through Ben, and now through the radio, and I told him I wasn't a kook and I didn't want to know my father.

I shrugged it off for as long as I could. I went on saying no to God, and I stopped holding my tongue. But the Voice came to me when I crossed the Bybee Bridge and when I went to sleep at night. The Voice said I was to find my father and go to him and sit across from him and tell him I forgave him.

I told God no again, but he came back to me and asked me if I really believed he could write a better story—and if I did, why didn't I trust him?

I didn't have an answer to that question. Why didn't I trust God? I believed he was the Writer who was not me and he could write a better story than I could, but I did not trust him.

Back then I was reading a devotional called *A Year of Days with the Book of Common Prayer* by Edmond Browning. One of his entries surprised me and for some reason helped me trust God. Browning said this:

I have the good fortune to be a grandfather. Twelve times. Oh, sure, I loved being a father. There were so many of us Brownings—Patti and I have five children—so much to keep track of with the comings and goings of all of them through the years, that I never really thought much about becoming a grandfather until the reality of it was almost upon me. I was unprepared for the emotional power of seeing that first tiny member of our next generation. I often wonder exactly what it is about the grandchildren that moves me so.

I fell asleep that night thinking about that passage, taking comfort in the fact that we change over time and our perspective sharpens with experience. I don't think Edmond Browning loves his grandchildren more than he loves his children, but I think he loves them differently. Perhaps he understands more acutely the importance of love and the beauty of life itself, the inestimable potency of beauty within the tiny newness of his grandchild. Being a grandfather, I think Edmond Browning must have felt more accurately what is important and what is not, and what was most important would have been love, the severe desire for the child, not to succeed, but to fearlessly engage in a world in which love is so fearfully exchanged. I would think he would want to whisper into the child's ear some magic words, and at the same time Browning must have felt the frustration Tolstoy knew all his days, ever searching for the green stick his brother hid in the woods at Yasnaya Polyana.

And then I thought about God, who was never born and will never die, and how many generations have gone before him, making him the Grandfather ad infinitum, and how this perspective would not be unlike Edmond Browning's, except multiplied by a thousand generations of new children come and gone, and the eternal experience of loving community before there were children at all. And I heard God's voice again that night, saying I should find my father. And this time I trusted him, and I knew he would guide me through a better story.

sixteen

Something on the Page

YOU'RE WRITING ANOTHER book about yourself?" Jordan asked. He was sitting at the counter in the kitchen eating a bowl of cereal. He had his laptop open and was choosing the starting lineup for his college fantasy basketball team. He'd been playing the game for a year and finally had a division one team. He said he was going to start his best defense, because defense wins championships.

"I'm not writing a book. I'm not talking about a book. I'm talking about me. I don't think I'm telling a good story."

"I think you tell good stories. Lots of people think so."

"I tell good stories in books. I don't live good stories."

Jordan poured more milk in his cereal. He was looking at me while pouring the milk. He was squinting his eyes a little and furrowing his brow. He stopped pouring the milk. He kept looking at me for ten seconds or more, like he was studying me.

"You're right," he finally said. "You aren't living a good story."

"That's what I was saying."

"I see," he said.

"What do I do about that?"

"You're a writer. You know what to do."

"No, I don't."

Jordan looked at me with his furrowed brow again. "You put something on the page," he said. "Your life is a blank page. You write on it."

Part
Three

A Character Who
Wants Something

seventeen

How to Make Yourself Write a Better Story

A LOT OF people think a writer has to *live* in order to write, has to meet people and have a rich series of experiences or his work will become dull. But that is drivel. It's an excuse a writer uses to take the day off, or the week or the month off for that matter. The thinking is, if we go play Frisbee in the park we're going to have a thousand words busting out of us when we get back to the house. We're going to write all kinds of beautiful prose about playing Frisbee. It's never worked for me. Annie Dillard, who won the Pulitzer while still in her mother's womb, wrote one of her books in a concrete cell. She says most of what a writer needs to really live they can find in a book.

People who live good stories are too busy to write about

them. Nobody ever strapped a typewriter to the back of an elephant and wrote a novel while hunting wild game. Nobody except for Hemmingway. But let's not talk about Hemmingway.

I only say this because part of the reason my life had become uninspiring is I'd sat down to earn a living. Literally, I sat in a chair and typed words. And that's fine, because I like the work, and it pays the rent. But Jordan was right: my life was a blank page, and all I was putting on the page were words. I didn't want to live in words anymore; I wanted to live in sweat and pain. I wanted some make-out sessions and perhaps a little trouble with the law. I wanted to find my dad, if for no other reason than to mark it off my to-do list. It kept bugging me.

But the want was not enough. My desire to live a better story didn't motivate me to do anything. I kept sitting down and writing more and more boring words into my life. And when I wasn't sitting down writing boring words, I was sitting down watching television. Steven King calls the television "the glass teat," and I was suckling on it for all its sugar. I was licking the glass and pawing at it like a kitten.

My friend Bob, the guy who writes down all his memories, hasn't seen a movie since *Who Framed Roger Rabbit*. No kidding. He's too busy living actual stories to watch them on a screen.

I suppose it was the conversation with Jordan that finally did it, that finally helped me understand how to tell a story with my life. It worked just like writing a book, you know. You just sit down and do the work as faithful as a plumber. You never feel like writing any more than a plumber feels like fixing a pipe, but just like him, you make a plan and start in on the messy work of making a story.

So that's when I started creating a few different stories at the same time. One story was about finding my father, the other was about chasing a girl, and still another was about, well, riding my bicycle.

That summer, the summer after the winter we started writing the movie, the Tour de France was being broadcast on television. And for some reason it affected me differently than watching other sports. I mean, when I watch football it doesn't make me want to play football, and baseball doesn't make me want to play baseball, but for whatever reason, watching Lance Armstrong win his seventh consecutive Tour de France made me want to ride a bike. I figure if a guy can be diagnosed with cancer and overcome cancer and then win seven Tours then start an organization trying to beat cancer itself, the least I could do would be to get off the couch. So I started riding a bike. Actually, I didn't really start riding a bike. I just kind of lifted my legs a little and made a circular motion with my feet while sitting in a chair watching the Tour d France. I made believe I was winning. Like I said, I live in daydreams.

●   ●   ●

Here's the truth about telling stories with your life. It's going to sound like a great idea, and you are going to get excited about it, and then when it comes time to do the work, you're not going to want to do it. It's like that with writing books, and it's like that with life. People love to have lived a great story, but few people like the work it takes to make it happen. But joy costs pain.

●　　●　　●

A general rule in creating stories is that characters don't want to change. They must be forced to change. Nobody wakes up and starts chasing a bad guy or dismantling a bomb unless something forces them to do so. The bad guys just robbed your house and are running off with your last roll of toilet paper, or the bomb is strapped to your favorite cat. It's that sort of thing that gets a character moving.

The rule exists in story because it's a true thing about people. Humans are designed to seek comfort and order, and so if they have comfort and order, they tend to plant themselves, even if their comfort isn't all that comfortable. And even if they secretly want for something better.

I heard an interview on the radio with a woman who worked with people in domestic abuse situations. She said most women who come to her for help go back to the situation they come out of, back to the man who abused them. When the interviewer asked why, the woman said that even though most women had family they could escape to and friends who would take them in, they returned to the abusive man because the situation, as bad as it might be, was familiar. People fear change, she said. Though their situations may be terrible, at least they have a sense of control; at least they know what to expect. Change presents a world of variables that are largely out of their control. And then the woman said this: "The women in these situations are afraid to choose a better story, because though their current situation might be bad, at least it's a *bad* they are familiar with. So they stay."

•   •   •

At the end of Act I of our screenplay, Don has to choose between a college he wants to attend and another his family wants him to attend, mostly because they'd offered a scholarship. It came time to move the story forward, and I recommended that Don get in his car and drive off to the school *he* wanted to attend, ignoring the demands of his family. Steve asked why Don would do this, and I said he would do this because he wanted to. It seemed obvious to me. But both Steve and Ben shook their heads.

"That's not how it works, man," Ben said, pushing his hair back and nodding. "Characters don't really choose to move. They have to be forced."

When he said that, I thought about those women I'd heard about on the radio.

"How do we get Don to go?" I asked Ben.

I was thinking about women, but I was also thinking about myself sitting in my chair watching the Tour de France, wishing I was out riding a bike, all the while completely able to ride a bike but for some reason not doing it. I thought about my father too, and how I wasn't moving on that story. And I thought about a specific girl I wasn't going after, and realized that the principle that characters do not want to change applies to more than fiction.

"We *make* him go," Ben said.

"We blow something up," Steve said. "We get somebody pregnant or drop a plane out of the sky."

"But that doesn't work in real life," I said.

Ben and Steve gave me a confused look. "We're not writing real life," Steve said.

"I know," I said, "right."

I stopped talking. I didn't want to explain. So Steve and Ben and I created an event in our story that forced Don to make a decision. It wasn't a real explosion, but it was a sort of social explosion, something that wouldn't allow him to stay in the same place anymore. He got in his car and drove away. Because of the explosion, he was beating the steering wheel with his fist when he drove away. Our story had started.

•　•　•

"Bourbon is whiskey made in Kentucky," Ben said.

"It's more than that," Jordan insisted. "It has to do with how they make it. One is made with oats and the other with wheat or something."

"Wheat's the same as oats," I said.

Steve said they aren't the same. "One makes oatmeal and the other makes bread."

Then Ben and I went out on the porch again, smoking our pipes. We were drinking bourbon, thinking about the screenplay. We were feeling about our characters as though we knew them, and we were somber a little because Don had left home. We knew he was going off on his story, probably to get hurt a little. We knew it would end well, but you don't feel that when you push a character into his story. You only feel what he is feeling at that moment.

Jordan came out to join us. He was wearing his ARMY shirt and the same sandals he always wears.

"It's going well?" Jordan asked.

"It's going fine," Ben said. "We just created our inciting incident."

"That's good," Jordan said. "It's all started now," he said, toasting us with his glass.

"So the inciting incident is when the plane falls out of the sky or something?" I asked for clarification. Ben looked at Jordan as though he couldn't say the answer exactly.

"It's just an event that forces your character to move," Jordan said, shrugging his shoulders.

Ben agreed. "It's the thing that happens to throw your character into their story."

"And that's how they change?" I asked.

Ben looked at me seriously, as though he wanted to ask

what I was really thinking about. But he didn't. Jordan said the story is what changes the character, not the inciting incident. "The inciting incident is how you get them to do something," Ben said. "It's the doorway through which they can't return, you know. The story takes care of the rest."

·   ·   ·

We'd watch movies when we weren't writing. We'd fall asleep in the living room with the fire going. I hadn't seen *Casablanca*, so Steve rented it at a video store on Woodstock. I laid down in front of the television and got lost in the story. It moves slower than modern stories, but I liked it. I liked the black and white, the softness around the characters, the actors moving around behind the principal characters like stage actors, moving around in exaggerated motions. I liked Rick, the way he talked to his friends as though he could crush them but chose to pro-tect them.

When Isla walked into the bar, I heard Ben say "inciting incident" under his breath. And it was true, because once she walked into the bar, Rick's life changed and there was nothing he could do about it. His girl was back, and he never thought he'd see her again. The inciting incident had disrupted his comfortable life, and he would naturally seek comfort again, thus creating a story from discomfort to comfort.

Robert McKee says humans naturally seek comfort and stability. Without an inciting incident that disrupts their comfort, they won't enter into a story. They have to get fired from their job or be forced to sign up for a marathon. A ring has to be purchased. A home has to be sold. The character has to jump into the story, into the discomfort and the fear, otherwise the story will never happen.

* * *

When Steve and Ben left, I watched the last week of the Tour de France. But I wasn't pedaling my feet in the air anymore. I went down to Veloce cycles and bought a bike. I bought some stupid pants to wear, and some shoes. It wasn't an inciting incident, exactly, but it was something. I needed something that would *force* me to ride the bike, and I started looking for whatever opportunity that might be. I pulled a group of friends together to ride in the Portland Bridge Pedal, eighteen thousand cyclists crossing all the major bridges in Portland, thirty miles, in the world's largest peloton. It was awesome. I'd executed a little inciting incident and lived a little story. I was *doing* something.

I didn't want to pretend anymore. I wanted to live some stories. I called my mom and asked her how long it had been since she'd heard from my father. We'd never talked about my father. In thirty years, we'd never spoken of him. She got quiet and then said she hadn't heard from him in decades. She said she feared he was dead. I asked if she had his Social Security number, and she said she might; she'd look.

None of this was an inciting incident, but speaking out loud about my father, just talking about him, was the start of something. I felt like a writer putting some characters on the page, playing with concepts, mapping out a story.

eighteen

An Inciting Incident

PERHAPS ONE OF the reasons I've avoided having a clear ambition is that second you stand up and point toward a horizon, you realize how much there is to lose. It's always been this way.

My friend Mike knows an ugly guy who dates beautiful women. He dates them for a while then moves on to other beautiful women. Mike looked at me and asked, "You know how he does it?" Mike said the way the guy did it is he didn't care whether he got rejected. He said only about one out of ten girls actually went out with the guy.

I don't want to date a bunch of beautiful women, because the pretty ones can be annoying. They stamp their feet and clench their fists because they can't have whatever the equivalent of a pony happens to be. But I do think there was something to what Mike was saying, that the great stories go to those who don't give in to fear.

The most often repeated commandment in the Bible is "Do not fear." It's in there over two hundred times. That means a couple of things, if you think about it. It means we are going to be afraid, and it means we shouldn't let fear boss us around. Before I realized we were supposed to fight fear, I thought of fear as a subtle suggestion in our subconscious designed to keep us safe, or more important, keep us from getting humiliated. And I guess it serves that purpose. But fear isn't only a guide to keep us safe; it's also a manipulative emotion that can trick us into living a boring life.

Shortly after Mike told me that, I noticed a girl who'd been hanging out in our group of friends. She was a friend of a friend, really, and had been showing up at the Lucky Lab on Wednesday nights where some of us were in the habit of getting together. She was cute and laughed a lot and wasn't frilly. I'd noticed her and talked to her a few times, but I was a bit afraid. She wasn't giving me any signals, you know.

So about this time a friend from Alabama e-mailed to say he was flying to Peru to hike the Inca Trail to Machu Picchu. He asked if I wanted to come and invited me to invite any of my friends too. I didn't research the hike or anything, and I was certainly in no shape to climb mountains, and like I said, if I was going to get into shape, I was going to do it through cycling. But the next week at the Lucky Lab I wanted to sound impressive, so I said I was thinking of going to Peru to hike the Inca Trail and wondered if anybody else wanted to come. This girl, the one who hadn't given me any signals, said she'd always wanted to do that hike, and a friend of hers said the same thing. And right then and there they said they wanted to come. "It's a date," I said, and got an odd look from across the table.

By the time I got home from the Lab, the girl had e-mailed confirming she was serious. So I e-mailed my friend in Alabama and said there would be three of us from Portland joining him and his friends in Peru. I think I was so excited about the girl that I forgot that I was in no shape to climb mountains. And the next day I looked up the Inca Trail on the Internet. The first article I found said the hike was extremely difficult, and a person should be in good physical shape before arriving in Peru. I read a description of the hike, and it turns out the Inca Trail climbs to 14,000 feet, then back down, then back up to 12,000 feet, then all the way back down to the Sacred Valley above which Machu Picchu sits in the clouds. I thought perhaps the warnings about physical fitness were exaggerated, so I googled "Inca Trail" and "excruciating" and read about fifty personal accounts of self-inflected Peruvian torture. I actually read warnings from people saying stay away, that even if you are a runner, the trail is extremely difficult. *What in the world have I gotten myself into?* I wondered. But it was too late. Without knowing it, I'd created an inciting incident. I'd told my friend I'd go, and I'd invited a girl I wanted to date. I was in a story.

James Scott Bell says an inciting incident is a doorway though which the protagonist cannot return. I didn't know I was doing it at the time, but I had certainly walked through a doorway. I was an overweight, out-of-shape guy who wanted to get into shape and date a specific girl. I'd walked through a doorway that would force me both to get into shape and to interact with her. I suppose I didn't *have* to get into shape, but if I didn't, the story would be a tragedy. And nobody wants to live a tragedy. I'd found my motivation. I joined a gym the next day.

nineteen

Pointing Toward the Horizon

YOU DON'T KNOW a story is happening to you when you're in it. You slide into the flow of it like a current in the ocean; you look back at the beach and can't see your umbrella, and your hotel is a quarter mile behind you.

The trainer at the gym was named Dave, and he was unlike any trainer I'd ever had. It wasn't the first time I'd joined a gym or the first time I'd had a trainer. I'd tried to get into shape a few times before, each time without a story to guide me, and each previous experience was a dismal failure. The trainer before Dave had been a young, pretty girl who hated men. On my first day at the gym, she worked me out so hard I could no longer lift an empty barbell. And the next day I couldn't get out of bed. Or the day after that, for that matter. And after a month I quit. I mean, why should I get into shape when there isn't a story giving me a good reason? But the situation was different now. I needed to get into shape because I didn't want to be humiliated in front of the girl. And I wanted that great ending, arriving at Macchu Picchu at sunrise, having crossed mountains to get there.

And Dave taught me a lot about living a good story. He taught me that progress, no matter how slow, is all that matters. On our first day we sat on the exercise bike and pedaled slowly for twenty minutes. If I pedaled too hard, he told me to slow down. And after twenty minutes he told me I was done and could go home. I asked him if he was serious, and he said he was. He said that twenty minutes of mild exercise should be considered a workout, and if I worked out five days a week, I should be completely satisfied. "You should never feel guilty for not doing anything beyond twenty minutes of mild exercise," he said. "Everything else is icing on the cake."

Then he said, "Tomorrow we put the icing on the cake."

The next day, he worked me out so hard I had to go into the alley behind the gym to throw up. "Remember," he said while I was dry-heaving against the wall, "this is all icing on the cake. Twenty minutes of light exercise is all it takes." I wiped my mouth and looked at him for compassion. He went back inside and came out with a medicine ball. He threw it at me. I rolled it back to him.

After a while the story about training for Peru was going

well. It was suspenseful, because I'd go work out with Dave, and every time I worked out, I'd feel out of shape, and that made me wonder whether I had what it took to finish the hike. Suddenly my life wasn't boring or meaningless. There was something I had to do in order to keep a bad thing from happening.

It's true that while ambition creates fear, it also creates the story. But it's a good trade, because as soon as you point toward a horizon, life no longer feels meaningless. And suddenly there is risk in your story and a question about whether you'll make it. You have a reason to get out of bed in the morning. I'd be lying if I said it was all fun. I definitely lost a few hours of sleep imagining myself collapsing on the Inca Trail, but it beat eating ice cream and watching television. I was doing something in real life. I'd stood up and pointed toward a horizon, and now I had to move, whether I wanted to or not.

I was watching the movie *Star Wars* recently and wondered what made that movie so good. Of course, there are a thousand reasons. But I also noticed that if I paused the DVD on any frame, I could point toward any major character and say exactly what that person wanted. No character had a vague ambition. It made me wonder if the reasons our lives seem so muddled is because we keep walking into scenes in which we, along with the people around us, have no clear idea what we want.

twenty

Negative Turns

I HAPHAZARDLY PURSUED my father. My mother gave me all the information she had, which wasn't much, and I wrote it on a sticky note that sat on the counter in the kitchen for a week. I thought about typing it into some database on the Internet, but I didn't know what database I should use, and I didn't bother trying to figure it out. I was still scared.

Like I said, watching a story is not the same as actually living a story. When you are watching a story you can watch a character struggle and enjoy it. But when you *are* that character, when you're actually living inside the story, it's not so fun. When I thought about my father, I got nervous and my mind raced. I suddenly wanted to mow the lawn or paint a room or rewire the dome light in my truck. What I didn't want to do was find my father.

My dad was a basketball coach when I was a kid. I remember visiting him at the high school where he worked, all the athletes running laps, my father standing in the middle of the gym with a whistle, prodding the team like a man training horses. And as I said, I grew up fat. I was losing a little weight training for the Inca Trail, but I was still out of shape.

• • •

I read a book a couple of years ago by Steven Pressfield called *The War of Art*. The book is about writing, about the process of getting words onto an empty page. Pressfield said a writer has to sit down every day and write, regardless of how he feels. He said you can sit around and wait for inspiration to come, but you'll never finish your book that way. "The muse honors the working stiff," Pressfield says. He also says that every creative person, and I think probably every other person, faces resistance when trying to create something good. He even says resistance, a kind of feeling that comes against you when you point toward a distant horizon, is a sure sign that you are supposed to do the thing in the first place. The harder the resistance, the more important the task must be, Pressfield believes.

If I learned anything from thinking about my father, it's that there is a force in the world that doesn't want us to live good stories. It doesn't want us to face our issues, to face our fear and bring something beautiful into the world. I guess what I am saying is, I believe God wants us to create beautiful stories, and whatever it is that isn't God wants us to create meaningless stories, teaching the people around us that life just isn't worth living.

I don't know why there are dark forces in the world, but there are. And I don't know why God allows dark forces to enter into our stories, but he does.

My friend, Kathy, had a hard relationship with God for a long time. She had a marriage go bad, and it went badly for a long time while it was going bad. Some hard things happened to her daughter because of this. Some of them happened at the same time the Rwandan genocide was happening, which made the whole world seem crazy. She wondered why it mattered if Jesus hung on a cross and died. Since the world went crazy anyway.

She hung out in the fringes of God for a while, and about a year ago she was ready to let go of God completely. Then she had a chance to go to Rwanda, with a small group of people. It felt personal, as if there was more to the story that had started so many years earlier, so she went. She spent some time in the countryside, and then went to the capital city, Kigali. They took a tourist bus to the genocide museum in Kigali.

Kathy got off the bus and made her way through the exhibits, reading about the events that led up to the genocide, the colonial rule, the confusion of identity created by British occupation, and the tribal tensions that mounted between the Hutus and the Tutsis. Churches got caught up in the genocide too. Kathy read the part about religion and was emboldened. "See," she prayed, "you created us only to let us march around in our own misery. You're supposed to be good. What are you good for?"

A twenty-minute ride away from the memorial is one of the genocide sites—a church where Tutsis had hidden from Hutus during the massacre. The Tutsis believed they would be spared if they took refuge in the church, but they weren't. The men came in with their machetes and slaughtered those hiding in the church. They cut the hands of the mothers who covered their children's faces, and they cut into the children's faces. The museum had piled the skulls against the wall and laid out the bones as a memorial.

Kathy took the tour bus to Ntarama. She walked into the church and looked at the bones lying cold on the iron rails. She looked at the ragged and bloody clothes hanging from the walls. She was ready to feel the same old anger at God, only a thousandfold more. She was ready to pray her last prayer, announcing that she could no longer believe in God in a world with such pain, with so much devastation.

But Kathy told me it was then and there, in that church, that she heard from God. Instead of the old anger, she felt overwhelming tenderness and sorrow.

This is what happens when people walk away from me, Kathy. I have brought you to this place to show you something important.

This is what happens when my compassion and love leave a place.
It is when people do not allow God to show up through them,
she realized, that the world collapses in on itself.

As Kathy told me the story, I thought about the resistance.
I thought about the fear of finding my dad, of talking to the
girl, of hiking the Inca Trail, and suddenly the resistance had a
darker feel, a thieving feel, as if something tangible and powerful were taking our beautiful stories away.

•   •   •

I kept walking past the sticky note on the kitchen counter; I
kept resisting my story. But you can only do that for so long.
It's true what Steven Pressfield says: there is a force resisting
the beautiful things in the world, and too many of us are giving in. The world needs for us to have courage, Robert McKee
says at the end of his book. The world needs for us to write
something better.

My friend Kaitie had a friend who worked in the district
attorney's office in Seattle. His job was to find people. I gave her
the information about my dad, and she e-mailed it to her friend.
I distracted myself. I mowed the lawn. I trimmed the hedges. I
ran an extension cord from the garage along the side of the
flower bed and out to the oak tree in the front yard. I ran the
cord up the trunk and out a limb then plugged an outdoor lan-
tern into the cord and hung it over the front steps. I bought an
issue of *Bicycle* magazine. I rode my bike into town and came

home and sat on a bag of ice for an hour. I kept googling "Inca Trail" and "excruciating" and then went to the gym, thinking about the blogs I'd read. And then I got the word.

Kaitie forwarded me the response from her friend in the DA's office. She figured it was personal and didn't read it before she sent it. But the man in the DA's office supposed Kaitie would filter it before giving me the news. My father had stayed in Houston, where I last saw him. He'd been within twenty miles of my home the entire time I was growing up. He'd died only five years earlier. "Your friend's father is deceased," the e-mail said. "I'm sorry about that."

•   •   •

A story is made up of turns, Robert McKee says. Once an ambition has been decided, a positive turn is an event that moves the protagonist closer to the ambition, and a negative turn moves the protagonist away from his ambition. All stories have both. If a story doesn't have negative turns, it's not an interesting story. A protagonist who understands this idea lives a better story. He doesn't give up when he encounters a setback, because he knows that every story has both positive and negative turns.

But what do you do when your ambition is no longer attainable? What do you do when your story ends just as it begins?

In a way, I have to confess I was relieved to hear my father had passed away. I didn't want to have to introduce myself having never accomplished anything remotely athletic. And I think the fact I'd never have to meet him helped me forgive him too. Without having to worry about what he would think of me, I was able to assume he had always wanted to make contact, and perhaps he'd even checked up on me from afar every once in a while. Maybe he was standing off in a field while I was at marching band practice. I remember the day I graduated from high school, wondering if he was up in the stands, feeling his eyes on me, scared even then that he would step out of the shadows. But now that he was dead, I was able to suppose he didn't care whether I was athletic or not. And then, to be honest, I missed him. I grieved the death of my father, I suppose. And it's an odd thing to grieve somebody you never knew.

But I was also proud of myself. And maybe that's the point of what I'm trying to say here. Maybe, I assumed, this was the only thing that would come out of this story, just the affirmation that I was somebody willing to do a bold thing.

Had he been alive, I would have gone through with it, I think. I think I would have called my dad and perhaps gone and seen him. Perhaps we would have become friends. I would have faced the resistance. Or at least I think I would have.

twenty-one

A Good Story, Hijacked

LAST YEAR, I had to go through all twelve months of my bank statements and highlight anything I could write off. At first I started the assignment sort of excited, because I thought I might save money on my taxes. As I highlighted potential business write-offs, however, I began to realize the stuff I spent money on indicated the stories I was living. By that I mean the stuff I spent money on was, in many ways, the sum of my ambitions. And those ambitions weren't the stuff of good stories.

I actually bought a Roomba vacuum cleaner, for example. I highlighted that line on my statement and then looked over at it sitting in the corner of the room. I'm not sure why I thought I needed a Roomba, but apparently I had nothing going on that day. I think I turned it on a couple of times just to see how it worked, and after that I forgot about it and used a broom. I'd bought a new truck that year, and I'd moved from a house to a much nicer condo. Nothing against a nice condo, but I privately wondered whether I was a protagonist telling an exciting story who happened to live in a nice condo, or whether I was a protagonist telling a boring story about trying to pay off his nice condo. Looking over my bank statements, I feared the latter might be true.

My only consolation was I wasn't alone. Most Americans aren't living very good stories. It's not our fault, I don't think. We are suckered into it. We are brainwashed, I think.

Last week I read an article in the paper that said the average American encounters three thousand commercial messages each day. It went on to discuss how advertising causes us to think in wish-fulfillment dynamics. The article was printed on a page across from a Best Buy ad announcing a sale on remote controls, including one that had a touch screen like an iPhone. The ad said the remote control could command all the electronics in your home. I had trouble finishing the article about the effects of advertising because I kept pressing my finger against the picture of the remote, imagining my television turning on and off.

Before I started writing for a living, I had a job as a marketing guy at a start-up company that sold textbooks to the education market. In learning about my job, I had to read all kinds of other books about how to sell people stuff they didn't need. As near as I could tell from reading those books, marketing is a three-step process. The first step is to convince people they are miserable. The second step is to convince people they will be happy if they buy your product, and the third step is to include a half-naked woman in your pitch. I read so many of these ideas I actually considered creating a magazine ad showing a teacher in a bikini draped seductively over a pile of geometry books.

The thing I never realized while I was studying marketing was the process of advertising products is, in many ways, a manipulation of the elements of story. It's like I was telling you about an inciting incident disrupting the stability of a character's life, throwing him or her into a story. Advertising does exactly this. We watch a commercial advertising a new Volvo, and suddenly we feel our life isn't as content as it once was. Our life doesn't have the new Volvo in it. And the commercial convinces us we will only be content if we have a car with forty-seven airbags. And so we begin our story of buying a Volvo, only to repeat the story with a new weed eater and then a new home stereo. And this can go on for a lifetime. When the credits roll, we wonder what we did with our lives, and what was the meaning.

It's all very seductive, and rather fascinating. I saw a commercial the other day for a dishwashing liquid. The opening scene showed a woman standing over a sink of greasy dishes, scrubbing hard against some dried-up lasagna that wouldn't come off a plate. Her hair was disheveled, the kids were running around in the kitchen, and her husband was probably off watching television. The woman standing over the dirty sink looked toward the heavens as though to cry out to God, "How can this be happening to me?" And then the new dishwashing liquid was introduced. There was a magic graphic about how the dishwashing liquid has little living bubbles that dissolve grime on contact. And after the magic bubbles were explained, we were back in the woman's kitchen. The woman's hair was done, she was down twenty pounds, the kids were doing their homework, and the husband was back in the picture, holding his arms around the woman's waist.

The cultural scripts running through that commercial are numerous, but the point of it seems much grander than a simple illustration of an effective dishwashing liquid. Actually, when you really break the commercial down, honestly looking at the subtext, the commercial seems to be saying something more direct: "If you use this dishwashing liquid, people will want to have sex with you."

I know for a fact it isn't true about the dishwashing liquid. I have three cases in my pantry.

I'm a sucker for this sort of thing, and apparently so are the rest of you.

The ambitions we have will become the stories we live. If you want to know what a person's story is about, just ask them what they want. If we don't want anything, we are living boring stories, and if we want a Roomba vaccum cleaner, we are living stupid stories. If it won't work in a story, it won't work in life.

*   *   *

The publishing company I work with is in Nashville, so I found myself there recently sitting with a group of publishers who looked confusingly at me when I told them I wanted to write a book about stories.

I tried my best to explain the concept, that all of us are living stories, and those stories teach other people to live stories. And what our stories are about matters, not just for us but for the world.

"You know," I said, "a story is based on what people think is important, so when we live a story, we are telling the people around us what we think is important." I said it just like that but in a more sophisticated way.

"Will the book have pictures in it?" one of the publishers asked, looking rather hopeful.

I sat back and tried to think of a way to illustrate my point.

A man named Jethro once lived on a quiet
farm with his wife, Marybelle, and their
young daughter, Amy Fae.

Jethro dreamed of a life larger than the one
he lived on the farm.

One day at church, Jethro heard his young
daughter sing with a beautiful voice.

So he took her to a recording studio in town.
The record executive thought he'd never
heard a voice so beautiful.

So the record executive made Amy Fae's voice even more beautiful with a computer program called Pro-Tools.

And the record executive gave Amy Fae a
bunch of new clothes to wear.

And the record executive changed Amy Fae's
name to Beat-Master Jane, a name Jethro
thought was lovely.

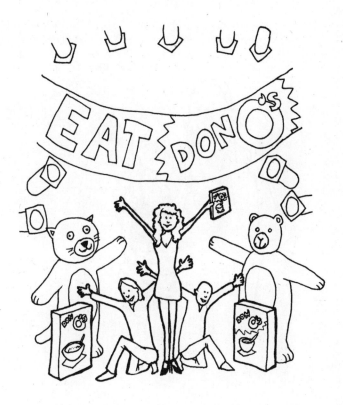

And a television producer gave
Amy Fae her own show on a cable channel
created specifically for children.

**And so Jethro and his new wife, Bambi,
lived happily ever after.**

twenty-two

A Practice Story

I KEPT RIDING my bike and icing my butt. There is a route I'd take from the condo to the river, then I'd take a paved trail into town where I looped along the waterfront, sitting up a little higher when pretty girls jogged past me. Whenever I got tempted to skip a workout, I'd google "Inca Trail" and "excruciating" again, and that was enough to get me into my workout clothes.

I'd ride my bike every day, then go hiking in the Columbia River Gorge every few days, climbing stairs or hiking the steep trail to Angels Rest. I was less winded every time I went out, and that was encouraging. But I still didn't think I was ready. The date came quicker than I wanted, but I packed my bags with pants a size smaller, a new backpack, and new-smelling gear from REI; and the girls and I boarded our flight out of Portland.

We flew the red-eye into Nicaragua, and the next morning boarded a flight to Lima. We stayed a night in Lima, then took a smaller plane into the Andes, high into the mountains to a town called Cusco, Peru. The plane descended so close to the mountains, to the jagged, snow-dusted knife blades of the Andes, I honestly thought we were going to crash. But it didn't matter. We were glued to the windows all the same, watching as the plane rocked back and forth over the high-sloped crops of corn and the pink roofs of the villages settled in the high meadows of Peru.

The girls and I arrived a day before the group from Alabama, so we walked around in the altitude, breathing heavy at the slightest hill, dry-mouthed and dry-eyed. Cusco is at eleven thousand feet, nearly as high as Mount Hood, the mountain I see every day in Portland, a mountain covered in snow nearly year-round. But Cusco is an arid mountain town, and warm year-round. It's on the equator, so the snow melts early, except in the highest elevations, and it stays gone for most of the year.

I spent a third of my time worrying about whether I'd be able to hike the trail, another third wondering about the girl I liked, and still another amazed by the beauty of Peru, especially the beauty of Cusco. The town square is walled on two sides by ancient cathedrals, and the restaurants that bank the other two sides provide balconies sitting and looking out over the women weaving their blankets and the children begging from the tourists who walk through the square, looking up at the cathedrals and the restaurants and the fountain in the middle of the square.

The girls and I climbed the stairs of a restaurant and sat out on the balcony overlooking the square. We ordered chicken and steak and tamales and corn grown on the high mountain slopes. The corn was as sweet as sugar and so juicy you nearly drank the kernels off the ear. There were women dancing in the square: older, stunted women, blocky with dark faces and black hair, and the blackest, most beautiful eyes. They were dressed in their bright, handmade clothes that shone brighter against their dark skin, and there were ribbons dangling off their palms. They were turning and dancing to the clapping of a drum. They were singing and laughing in the shadow of the cathedrals and in the sound of the water pouring off the fountain. The girls and I leaned over to see them better and to parse the words to their Spanish songs. Two police came up shyly and stepped into the dancing and explained to the women that they had to stop dancing in the square.

"No!" we shouted to the police. "Let them dance!"

The women pointed to us on the balcony, saying the Americans wanted to see them dance. The policemen waved their hands to dismiss us, then folded their hands together as though to beg the women to stop dancing in the public square.

"No!" we shouted again. "Let them dance!"

The policemen showed us their palms and dropped their hands, then walked away, shaking their heads. The women continued dancing, waving their ribbons toward us, sliding their feet along the brick square to the sound of the clapping drum and the fountain.

●　●　●

It's hard to sleep at eleven thousand feet. There isn't much oxygen, and there was pollution from the cars, from the broken mufflers of cabs running up and down the thin streets of Cusco. Even after midnight the exhaust was coming in through the open windows of our hostel. My eyes felt too large in their sockets, and the back of my throat felt as if it had been rubbed down with a dry cloth. The three of us were in one room, each sleeping on a bed smaller than the one I'd slept on as a child. A Catholic woman with thoughtful eyes had checked us in and looked the other way when the three of us put our bags into one room. I was against the wall, and the girl I liked slept in the bed next to me. She had a lovely nose, I remember thinking, and even though the air was thin, she slept with her mouth closed. Her hand lay open and faced down against the sheet by her pillow. I had been watching her for ten minutes or so when she opened her eyes and saw me looking at her. I closed my eyes. I rolled over and faced the wall, and in another hour, fell asleep.

● ● ●

We started low in the Sacred Valley, along a river that ran through a desert canyon. Above us were the snow-covered steeples of the Andes, and beneath the peaks, high enough to find the sun, the farmers cut the steep land for their crops. They hiked up every day to their high fields. They hiked with their tools and their baskets for harvesting, straight up a thousand feet of trail, to tend their family business.

We were small among the giant mountains, our feet dragging through the deep sand along the river. We climbed for a few hours out of the canyon, along the ridge, until we arrived at a set of switchbacks that would begin the miles and miles of rock stairs leading to Machu Picchu. Our guide, Carlos, called us off the trail to a plateau where we looked over the river, now thousands of feet below, onto an ancient Inca ruin that would be the first of many long abandoned stone villages we would pass. He said it was a farming village, a stop on the way to Machu Picchu. Carlos said if we would have stayed on the trail along the river, Machu Picchu was only six hours away. In ancient times, the river was used as a commercial route, Carlos said, but if you visited Machu Picchu on a pilgrimage, you had to take the Inca Trail. When he said this, he pointed toward the Andes, up toward the snow, above the thick trees and the rain forest that rests above the desert valley. Then he said we would take four days to get there.

"Why would the Incas make people take the long route?" my friend from Alabama asked.

"Because the emperor knew," Carlos said, "the more painful the journey to Machu Picchu, the more the traveler would appreciate the city, once he got there."

We stood there appreciating the universal significance of what Carlos had said. There wasn't a person among us who wanted to take the shorter route. Except me, perhaps, but I didn't say anything. I just stood there looking appreciative like the rest of them.

From the plateau it was seven miles of climbing stairs. I found a rhythm and kept my head down and drank lots of water and ended up keeping with the group. I was surprised I could do it, but I could. I was a better hiker than I thought. When you've lived countless stories in which you play a sedentary role, it's an odd feeling to switch stories. But I was surprising myself.

That night we made camp a couple of thousand feet up the climb to Dead Woman's Pass. This pass would be the highest summit we'd ascend on the hike, just shy of 14,000 feet, nearly as tall as Mount Rainier in Washington state. We were well beneath the summit, though, and you could see the face and nose of the pass's namesake, her breast pointing toward the heavens. You could see her, only she was farther than in the pictures I'd seen; she was higher in the clouds. And because we got to camp before sunset, you could see the hikers along the gully leading up the pass. You couldn't see them at first, but if you looked closely, you thought you saw the ground moving along the crack in the mountain. The hikers looked like ants streaming toward the peak, ants in red jackets and yellow fleeces leaning into each step and rocking and stopping and then moving again.

My friend from Alabama stood next to me and shook his head. "What have we gotten ourselves into?" he asked.

"We should have followed the river," I said.

From our camp we hiked through dense rain forest, a microclimate that had developed along the stream that fell steeply in waterfalls down the mountain, back toward our previous night's camp. The trail turned to rock, to stairs cut and formed by an ancient civilization that did not use a wheel. Each of these massive stones was carried to its place on a man's back. And the steps were not small steps. Some of them were two feet high.

After the rain forest, the landscape opened up again, and we became the ants being watched by hikers making camp in the meadows beneath the pass. We were leaning into our steps now, not so much sore or exhausted as dead in our legs and working only because we'd no option but to continue. But the woman who lay on the mountain seemed as far now as she had hours before. And the people above us in the crag were just as small as they'd seemed to be the previous night. But we kept moving, without stopping, without breaking, and in three more hours we were within a hundred yards of the summit.

Some of my friends from Alabama had finished first, and the two girls I came with had finished, and they were sitting on rocks and cheering us on. I came up over the top of the summit, not smiling, embarrassed because the group was making such a noise about it. But I greeted them and turned and looked down the miles and miles of Peru that sat between the peak and where we'd come from. I'd not felt such a feeling of accomplishment in my life.

We stayed there, the highest point I'd ever been, in so many ways. We stayed there and took pictures on the rocks, on the surface of the gray moon of Dead Woman's Pass. We looked down on our camp on one side of the mountain and then turned and looked down at the camp we'd be staying at that night. We stayed until Carlos said we had to go, that the weather was turning and we needed to get out of the altitude.

*   *   *

The next day we summitted another pass, then hiked back down into the Sacred Valley. We hiked from before sunrise till after sunset, arriving at camp by flashlight. There was a building at our final campsite, and a restaurant where we ordered beers and food. Our porters lined up, and we thanked them and they thanked us. We gave them a huge tip, and one of us gave a speech and one of them gave a speech. We went to bed that morning only four miles from the Sun Gate, the overlook that rests above Machu Picchu.

We didn't hike to the Sun Gate the next morning; we ran. We ran on blistered feet and sore legs. We got there, and it was fogged in, so we sat along the rock, on the ruins, and waited for the fog to burn off. We sat and sang songs. And it was like Carlos said, because you can take a bus to Machu Picchu; you can take a train and then a bus, and you can hike a mile to the Sun Gate. But the people who took the bus didn't experience the city as we experienced the city. The pain made the city more beautiful. The story made us different characters than we would have been if we had skipped the story and showed up at the ending an easier way.

We walked among the ruins in the fog all morning, in the footsteps of the Inca's. We ran our fingers along the perfectly sculptured rock used to create the walls of their dwellings, rocks cut square to sit on rocks cut square, all built without mortar.

It wasn't only the pain of the trail that made you appreciate the city; it was the pain of the landscape, steep in the mountains of the Andes, spiraled towers of natural rock, cliffs dropping for a thousand feet to the river. And the houses, the weight of them and the perfection of their lines, spoke of the many dead Incas who gave their lives to build the city.

The pain made the city more beautiful. The story made us different characters than if we'd showed up at the ending an easier way. It made me think about the hard lives so many people have had, the sacrifices they've endured, and how those people will see heaven differently from those of us who have had easier lives.

In more ways than I can count, my practice story had changed me. I no longer thought of myself as incapable of hard physical challenges, and I wasn't watching much television anymore. I was chasing a girl now, and it was going well.

---

twenty-three

A Positive Turn

I DON'T KNOW if anybody actually writes his or her own story in real life. It's an odd thing to talk about, because while we control our destiny, it's limited control in so many ways. What makes a story work on the screen is the endless scenarios that might befall a protagonist. He may want the girl, but the girl may want somebody else, or she may leave the country or die. A writer of fiction can control all those elements, but as real-life protagonists we can control only what we do and say, what choices we make, what words we say. The rest is up to fate. And so life has positive and negative turns. And you rarely see them coming.

My mother called shortly after I got back from Peru. I hadn't told her about my father, her former husband. I hadn't told her he was dead—didn't know how to tell her, exactly. It had been a month, and I still wasn't finished grieving, and because my mother and I had never talked about him, I wasn't sure how she would react. She hadn't interacted with him in more than twenty years, after all, and because I never knew them as a married couple, I hadn't processed the idea she might grieve his loss too.

"I know you are looking for your father," she said over the phone. "I'm sorry we never talked about him. He wasn't a bad man. You would like him, you know." I was driving over the Bybee Bridge into Eastmoreland, on the way to a friend's house for dinner.

"I'm sure I would have, Mom. It's okay that we've never talked about him."

"Well, would you like to know him?" she asked. I wasn't sure what to say. If I went any further into the conversation, I'd be withholding the news that he was dead.

"I'm not sure what to say, Mom," I said after a pause.

"That's understandable," she said. "But I did find him. He lives in Indiana. I called him and talked to him and he said he'd like to meet you. I am going to leave the rest up to you."

"Pardon me?" I asked. I pulled the car over to the shoulder.

"I have his phone number and his address," she said. "I found a file I hadn't seen in years. It had some documents, his birth certificate and a Social Security card, and I found him on the Internet. Like I said, I talked to him, and he's open to meeting you."

"Mom. I . . ."

"That's okay. You don't have to say anything."

"You don't understand. I searched for him with the information you gave me earlier. He's dead. I got the e-mail a few weeks ago."

"No, Son. That's not true. Not sure why you heard that. I talked to him on the phone. He's very much alive."

I hung up the phone after a few more minutes and sat in my car looking out at the golf course. I watched a woman coming up from the distance, walking a dog, and I waited to feel something. But I didn't feel anything. Not at first. And so I drove to my friend's house, and when I turned off the car and put my fingers on the handle to get out of the car, I started trembling. I was short of breath. I still don't know what I was feeling, but I was certainly feeling something. I went into my friend's house, and they must have thought I was on drugs because I hardly talked and hoped everybody else would talk, and I sat quietly in my chair, my hand shaking, my spoon rattling against a bowl of soup.

* * *

I had his phone number in my wallet, but I didn't call him. A month went by, and I didn't call him, and then another month. I had a trip to Chicago on my schedule, and I told myself that when I went to Chicago I'd call and I'd cross the border into Indiana to see him. But the first night in Chicago, I didn't call, and the next night I didn't call. It came down to my last day, and I knew I had to do something. I knew I needed an inciting incident, something to make me jump into the story. So I sent out a text message to ten friends, telling them I was going to see my father, whom I hadn't seen in thirty years. And the text messages flooded back: prayers, encouraging verses, digital support followed by forests of exclamation points.

I called that morning and was relieved to get his voice mail. I told the man that I was his son and that I was coming to see him, driving from Chicago. I told him I'd be there within a few hours, though I hadn't looked at a map, so I wasn't sure. My voice must have been shaking on the phone. I told him to call me and let me know if he would be home, and if he wasn't going to be home, I'd turn around and go back to Chicago. I got in my rental car and entered his address into my GPS, and that's when I found out Indiana is larger than I thought. It would be a six-hour drive, and another six hours back. And so it was six hours of thinking about my father, of trying to figure out what I was feeling. I knew I had to go through with it. All my friends would ask that night, and the next day, and there was no way I could let them down. I didn't want to be known as a coward.

A couple hours into the drive, my father called. I didn't answer. I let it go to voice mail, and when he was done, I listened to the message on speakerphone. He had a deep voice, deeper than I remember but oddly familiar. I imagine it will be like that when we finally hear God's voice, it will be deep and familiar, and we will be interested and terrified. My father's voice seemed to come from a time before I existed, before time itself even. I pulled my car over again, and my hand was shaking. As eighteen-wheelers sped by on the highway, I looked out at a field and wished I could go into the field and throw up. I wanted to throw up and get rid of the shakes the way I'd done every time I had the flu. But I didn't get out of the car, and I didn't throw up. I got a text message from my friend Jena Lee saying she was praying for me, and I started the car and pulled back onto the highway and followed the trucks toward southern Indiana.

*   *   *

All I had to do was knock on the door, then do a handshake and some small talk. I just had to make my body go through the motions. I needed to check this off my to-do list. Meet my father. I didn't have any questions for him. In six hours of driving, I hadn't thought of a single question. I didn't want to be close to him. I didn't want to be friends. It's not that I didn't like him or hadn't forgiven him; I didn't know him and wasn't sure what there was to forgive him of in the first place.

I'm tall, but he was taller, and still barrel-chested like he was when I was young. He had all his hair and had a fraction of my smile. I look more like my mother, and my sister looks more like my father. He opened the door and smiled with my smile and stood back and looked at me and put his arms around me as though we hadn't seen each other in a few months. He told me to come in and pointed at the couch. He sat down in his chair, the television tuned to CNN, and leaned back and stared at me. I didn't stare back at him the way he looked at me. I looked at him more like a stranger at a meet and greet, somebody who wanted to tell me my books helped him figure out some bit of life, some hard moment. My mother had told him I was a writer, and I saw a copy of my book on the dining room table. He didn't know, however, that only a few months earlier, I'd released a book about growing up without a father and had talked about him in the book, and if he went down to his local bookstore, he could pick it up and read about himself.

He asked a few questions, but my answers were short. When I wouldn't talk, he talked. He offered me a beer and sipped his own and never turned off the television but talked over it about what his life was like when he was married to my mother. "It's different now," he said. "I'm different now." My father had remarried and had remained married for more than twenty years. I had a half brother who was a basketball player and, apparently, another half brother in Florida who was part-Cuban. I imagined myself part-Cuban. I pictured myself driving a '54 Pontiac through Havana, with a plate of *plátanos* on the dash.

He talked about when I was a kid, how he took my sister and me on a road trip to see his parents. We were just tiny, he said. He asked if I remembered, but I told him I didn't. He said surely I remembered, but I told him I didn't remember. He offered another beer, and I said no, and he drank another one himself, and with each beer he got louder than the television and friendlier, and as he talked, I liked him immensely. He'd moved back to Houston when my mother left Indiana. He'd moved back to town to be near us, and he asked if I remembered coming to his apartment when I was a kid. I told him I remembered. He said those were special times, and I agreed they were, though I also remember them being frightening times, only because I felt as though my mother had left me with a babysitter who was a man that coached basketball and left curly hairs in the bathtub after he took a shower.

"We lived here, in Indiana, when you were a child. You didn't know that, did you?" he asked.

"I didn't," I said. I knew, but I didn't have specific memories. I didn't want to explain that I'd seen pictures and that Mom had talked about Indiana, and those were my only points of reference.

"We lived here, but it didn't work," he said. "It got bad; the marriage got bad. We fought a lot, and then we decided to end it. I didn't want to end it, but it's all we could do. I cried, Son. I cried in front of the judge when he asked whether I wanted a divorce. I didn't want to leave you. It was not all my fault, but a lot of it was."

"I understand," I said.

"I loved her, you know, but it's just that, well, it's just—things got complicated. Man, I don't know. I'm Catholic. I'm Catholic and don't get divorced."

"I see," I said. And I was glad he'd had so many beers. I was glad something was making him comfortable talking, because I needed to hear what he was saying, and I don't think he would have said it if he were sober.

"So I went to Houston when your mother left. And I stayed in your lives. But it got hard. I couldn't do it. I couldn't stay anymore. I met this other girl, and we just started over. And I didn't make the same mistakes. I learned."

"That's good," I said. "I'm glad."

We were two hours into our conversation now, but he was coming to what he wanted to say. And I never thought there was anything he would have wanted to say. I never thought he would be nervous or scared, but he was both nervous and scared. He got tender, and there were tears in his eyes. He put his beer down, but he didn't turn down the television. Anderson Cooper was talking ethanol legislation; he was talking with a senator from Illinois.

"I don't have any excuses, Son," he said to me. And it was odd to be called *Son* by a man I hadn't seen in thirty years. It was odd to be anybody's son. It felt right, but right for another time and another place and another story that never actually happened.

"I'm sorry," he said. And he cried. A tear came down his cheek, and he put down his beer and reached his hand over the arm of his chair to the couch, and I took his hand. "I'm sorry," he repeated, his voice breaking with emotion. "Do you forgive me?"

"I do," I said. "I forgive you." And I did, even though I didn't know I needed to. I forgave him and haven't felt anything against him since. He took a sip from his beer and thanked me. He put his hand on my knee and squeezed till I thought my leg would break. He reached over and picked up my book and smiled and shook his head. "You can write," he said in a voice that seemed to come from before time. "I can't believe how good your stories are." I didn't want his words to mean anything. I didn't want to *need* his affirmation. But part of our *selves* is spirit, and our spirits are thirsty, and my father's words went into my spirit like water.

twenty-four

Meeting Bob

SOMETHING CHANGED AFTER I visited my father. Perhaps it was visiting my father and hiking the Inca Trail too. I was living a story, a life designed and lived with intention. I was watching less television and enjoying being in better shape. I had a long way to go on all fronts, but story was certainly making life a more enjoyable experience.

It was good to be pursuing a girl too. We were dating, actually, and I liked her, and sharing a story with somebody made the story more meaningful. I'd heard that in a movie, that other people testify that our lives are actually happening. It felt like that, I think. It felt as though I was designing stories for us, not just me.

And I found myself wanting even better stories. And that's

the thing you'll realize when you organize your life into the structure of story. You'll get a taste for one story and then want another, and then another, and the stories will build until you're living a kind of epic of risk and reward, and the whole thing will be molding you into the actual character whose roles you've been playing. And once you live a good story, you get a taste for a kind of meaning in life, and you can't go back to being normal; you can't go back to meaningless scenes stitched together by the forgettable thread of wasted time. The more practice stories I lived, the more I wanted an epic to climb inside of and see through till its end.

●　　●　　●

Steve and Ben were back in Portland, and the weather had turned warm. We were walking around a college near my condo, scouting the campus for places we could shoot our movie. The screenplay was nearly finished, and a company was trying to raise the money we needed to shoot the film, so we were on our way. I asked Steve if he thought we had a good movie, and he said he did. He said he thought it was a coming-of-age film, a movie millions of people would identify with and find comfort in.

"Do you think we will win an Academy Award?" I asked.

"No," he said, and he smiled when he said it. "I don't think we will win an Academy Award. Not anytime soon."

"So it's not a great story," I said.

Steve disagreed with that. He said it was a great movie,

but it wasn't an epic movie; it wasn't an over-the-top movie. He said our film was a comedy, and comedies almost never win Academy Awards. And he said our movie was subtle and gentle, a good independent film; and subtle and gentle movies rarely win best picture.

"What kind of things go into an epic movie?" I asked, perhaps letting on that I wasn't talking about movies anymore. Steve stopped walking and looked at me sincerely. He folded his clipboard in his arms and thought for a moment.

"Well," Steve said, "you're talking about taking a story to the next level. I think there are a couple things that take a movie into the category of epic." He started walking again, explaining what made a story great, while pointing out good places to shoot specific scenes in our film.

According to Steve, a story goes to the next level with two key elements, and both of them have to do with the ambition of the character. First, he said, is the thing a character wants must be very difficult to attain. The more difficult, the better the story. The reason the story is better when the ambition is difficult, Steve said, is because there is more risk, and more risk makes the story question more interesting to an audience. The greatest stories, Steve told me, are the ones in which the character's very life is at stake. There needs to be a question as to whether the character will make it, whether he will defeat the enemy or the enemy will defeat him.

The second element that makes a story epic, he said, was

the ambition had to be sacrificial. The protagonist has to be going through pain, risking his very life, for the sake of somebody else. "Those stories are gold," Steve said. "You can ask people to name their favorite movies, and those two elements will be in almost all of them."

And so that's when I realized what was missing from the Inca Trail story, and also from the story of meeting my father. It was certainly difficult, but in the end it was just a story about a good vacation, and the story of facing something difficult. Those are great stories, and I'll live stories like that for the rest of my life. But if I hadn't gone to Peru, nobody would have died. And if I hadn't seen my father, the fate of thousands would not have been affected. I don't mean to downplay the experiences, because they got me off the couch and got me to turn off the television, and my life certainly didn't feel meaningless anymore. But as I said, I wanted more. I didn't want to go to Scotland and fight the English for state sovereignty. Not yet, anyway. But I did want a next step, and Steve was laying out the conditions.

●　　●　　●

About that time my assistant, Tara, forwarded me an e-mail from my friend Jena, who runs an organization out of Nashville, an organization that drills freshwater wells in Sub-Saharan Africa. The e-mail said they were organizing a group of riders to ride bikes from Los Angeles to Washington, D.C., raising money and awareness about the global need for clean water. At first I thought the idea was absurd. The longest I'd ridden my bike was fifteen miles. The trip across America would be about three thousand miles farther, riding all day, six days a week, for nearly two months. I wondered when the riders would have time to ice their butts. But the more I thought about the trip, I realized it had all the makings of a better story. It would be extremely difficult, and it was certainly for a good cause. But when I imagined the other cyclists having to wait for me as I drank from people's lawn sprinklers, I opted out.

About that time, though, some old friends decided to kayak up the Jervis inlet in British Columbia. The trip would take about a week, and we'd be paddling about fifty miles to the back of the inlet, where there was a Young Life camp, before we'd turn around and paddle back. Even though it wasn't for a good cause, I signed up to go. I considered it another practice story, you know. And it also got my mind off that cycling trip. I figured if I did something else mildly athletic, I could stop the voices in my head accusing me of being a wimp.

In the Jervis inlet, the stone faces of the mountains come into the water like walls. You paddle down the mile-wide inlet with cliffs on either side, and the trees are lined up atop the cliffs like guardians of all the beauty.

On our first night on the water, we camped on one of the few beaches that wasn't taken by a cliff. In the night, there were no lights on the horizon, no civilization. There was no man-made noise, save the occasional passing yacht heading to Chatterbox Falls at the back of the inlet. And in the morning I found bald eagles nesting in a tree near our camp, and the seals would come up near our rocks and look at each other and sink back into the sea, coming up again a few yards farther as though they wanted us to chase them. The beauty of the inlet was nearly that of Peru, and I wondered at all this exposition God had created, as though it were an invitation to an epic so grand it might match the scenery. *The mountains themselves call us into greater stories,* I thought.

· · ·

A couple nights later, after kayaking through the rain for three cold, wet days, we made our camp near Chatterbox Falls. The falls clapped against the inlet in so much thunder, like a thousand people clapping, a standing ovation. Down from the falls we made camp, and I sat on the rocks by the water and wondered what sort of story I'd tell with my life. The thing about writing a story, in real life and on paper, is half the effort is just figuring out what the story is going to be. I mean, half the writing process involves sitting in front of a whiteboard, waiting for ideas to come. And that's what the kayak trip felt like to me. It felt like quiet meditation and prayer.

· · ·

As I've said before, the main way we learn story is not through movies or books; it's through each other. You become like the people you interact with. And if your friends are living boring stories, you probably will too. We teach our children good or bad stories, what is worth living for and what is worth dying for, what is worth pursuing, and the dignity with which a character engages his own narrative.

There's no way I could have anticipated the positive turn that would take place next. We were fifty miles from the nearest road, after all. But the next morning, I met the greatest real-life storyteller I will, perhaps, ever know, a person who has forever adjusted my moral compass and destroyed all the bridges leading back to a common life. That person was Bob, the guy I've told you about a few times, the guy who has written down more than five hundred pages of memories.

We broke camp, packed our boats, and began paddling for home. But before crossing the inlet, our guide wanted to show us a lodge a man had built the previous year, a massive house set on a ledge just off the water. I thought it was odd that anybody would build a house back there, since you could only get to the place by seaplane or boat. But indeed, a home had been built. And it was an enormous and beautiful place, snug against the gray cliff of the mountain, with decks cascading down to the waterfront where there was a dock and some boats and a plane. The man was a lawyer, one of my friends said, who lived in San Diego but had a law firm in

Seattle. He was also the American consul to Uganda. He gives most of his money away, my friend said. He'd actually bought five thousand acres in the area to save the trees and preserve the beauty. We were only going to paddle by and take a look at the house; but as we got closer, we saw a man coming down the steps to the dock. "That must be him," my friend said. "That must be Bob."

By this time Bob had a *Great Gatsby* impression in my mind. He walked down the stairs to the dock and smiled and pulled his gray hair back and waved at us in large, graceful swings. He waved at us then with both hands to call us closer to the dock. And he was shouting something. "What's he saying?" one of my friends asked, pulling his paddle from the water.

"Are you hungry?" we heard Bob shout.

"He's asking us if we're hungry," my friend said. "Are we?"

"I think we are," I said. So we paddled toward Bob's dock.

As we got closer, Bob's sons came down the stairs and helped bring the boats to the dock. They held them and tied them to the dock as we climbed onto the dock.

Bob got down on his knees and helped us out as though we were expected guests, as though he'd been waiting a week for our arrival. "We saw you coming, and Sweet Maria put fruit out on the table," he said. "There's plenty. And she made lemonade too. Let's go up to the house and get you guys fed."

At first I thought Sweet Maria was the maid or something, but it turns out Sweet Maria is Bob's wife. When he talked about her, he nearly always called her Sweet Maria. And she was sweet too. She'd put fifty pounds of fruit on a large table on the main deck, and pitchers of water and lemonade, crackers and cheese, and fresh bread. The family was going back and forth to the kitchen, bringing out more food. I felt as though we'd found the Swiss family Robinson, as though Disney had dropped these people off to film a movie and forgot to take them back when they'd shut down production.

We were in a terrible condition to visit anybody. We were wet and hadn't showered in days. Because it had been raining on the inlet, we'd not been able to dry off, so our clothes smelled as if sea animals had died in our socks and our pockets. But Maria kept putting out fruit and welcoming us and gave us fresh towels to dry off. Then the sun came out, and we sat on the deck and talked with the Goffs. For the better part of an hour, they asked where we'd come from and what we did back home. Bob asked about our journey. He said he couldn't believe we'd paddled that far and that it took plenty long in a boat with a motor. I asked Bob how he'd come to build a lodge sixty miles from the nearest road, and he told us he'd grown up going to the Young Life camp nearby and always loved the place. He said the real reason for the lodge was to host leaders from foreign countries and talk about peace, to talk about how leaders can bring peace to their countries.

I was curious about how he got world leaders to fly into the middle of nowhere to talk about peace. Bob smiled and looked at his wife and said, "Well, now, that's an interesting story. I suppose we stumbled into that one, didn't we?"

Bob looked out at the inlet, trying to organize the story in his mind. When his children were young, he told us, he was spending time in Uganda, helping the government work through some legislation, and they asked him if he would be willing to serve as the American consul, essentially Uganda's official American lawyer. Bob agreed; but while he was a good lawyer, he'd never had to interact with diplomats.

On the flight home, he wondered what he'd say if he had to meet with the president of South Africa or the ambassador from France. When his kids asked how the trip went, he told them he'd been asked to serve as Uganda's official lawyer, and he was a little nervous to meet the dignitaries. So Bob asked the kids what they would say if they had to meet with the leader of a foreign country. Adam, the youngest, said he'd ask them if they wanted to sleep over. Bob said that was a terrific idea, because when people sleep over you get to know them really well. Lindsey said she'd want to ask them what they put their hope in, and Bob and Maria agreed that was a beautiful and important question. Richard, the oldest, who had recently been given a video camera, said he'd want to record the interviews so he could make a movie. Bob and Maria thought that was a terrific idea too. Bob said that if he ever met with a foreign leader, he'd remember their suggestions. But after thinking about it, Bob decided that the suggestions were too good to risk to chance.

"Let's write letters," Bob said. The kids wondered what their dad was suggesting. "I'm serious," Bob said. "Let's write all the leaders in the world and ask if they want to come over for a sleepover, and if we can interview them and ask what they hope in." The kids got very excited. Maria smiled and loved the idea. Bob told the kids that if any of the world leaders said yes to the interview, even if they couldn't come for a sleepover, he'd fly them to that country and they could video tape Lindsey asking what they hope in.

Bob didn't expect anybody to write back, so he brought home more than a thousand pieces of stationery and the kids researched world leaders and came up with more than twelve hundred addresses for heads of state and assistants. For a while they heard nothing, and Bob confessed he was relieved, but then a single letter came in, and a few days after, another. Both of them granting an interview. And then another letter, until in all twenty-nine world leaders contacted the Goffs instructing them on how to make arrangements to interview their countries leader. Bob shrugged his shoulders when he told us the story.

He put his family on planes, flying them all over the world. The kids' teachers were furious, saying that he was harming his children by taking them out of school. But Bob convinced them that his children might learn more interviewing the president of Paraguay than by reading a book about him, and the teachers reluctantly agreed.

Bob said the world leaders fell in love with his kids. He said there was no way he could have received as much hospitality on his own. Maria described one meeting in which the kids were waiting in the giant hall of a palace, sitting at a table for fifty, when the president walked in the room, stiff and formal. He leaned over and shook each of the children's hands without smiling. The children were intimidated by the man and didn't smile either. The president then asked the children if they wanted a glass of milk or a cookie. And the kids said they would, thank you. The man clapped his hands, and doors flew open, and teams of servants flooded into the room, holding trays of cookies and trays of milk, setting them on the table in front of the children and their wide eyes. The president laughed and opened his arms and told the children they were welcome in his country. At the end of each interview, Adam presented the world leader with a box that had a key in it, explaining that the key was an actual key to their family home in San Diego. He said they sometimes lock the door when they go to the store, but that he could just let himself in, and that if he ever wanted to have a sleepover, he was welcome in their home.

The relationships the family began that year would sustain. The world leaders wrote the children letters, and the children wrote back. And one world leader even came to San Diego and used his key and stayed over with the Goff family.

That year Bob said he learned people are just people, even if they are world leaders. He said most people want what's best for their friends and their families, and if they are given the opportunity to talk out their differences, they will. And so when the law firm did very well one year, he bought the land around the lodge and built a place for world leaders to come and have a sleepover.

"And they come?" I asked.

"We've had a few," Bob said. "I hang their flags from the banister, and we sit and eat and talk. We explore the inlet on the boats and usually do a little cliff jumping."

I tried to imagine a foreign diplomat jumping from one of the cliffs around the inlet. I smiled even thinking about it. Bob said that before the dignitaries leave, they sit and write a peace treaty, just some informal language that commits to making the world a better place, about how they will live sacrificially and try to do things for others as often as possible. He said each of the leaders signs the treaty and takes a copy home to remember their time at the lodge.

Bob and Maria's kids, now grown and in high school and college, each have a quiet dignity and confidence. They also have an informal charm, as though they just know they would like us if we'd take the time to get to know each other. It is obvious they'd played the roles in the story their family was living, the roles of foreign dignitaries, traveling with their parents on the important assignment of asking world leaders what they hope in. Their *story* had given them their *character*.

I only say this about the children because I used to believe charming people were charming because they were charming, or confident people were confident because they were confident. But all this is, of course, circular. The truth is, we are all living out the character of the roles we have played in our stories.

●　　●　　●

Maria and the kids came down with desserts, pastries they'd baked while we'd been talking out on the deck. Bob gave me a walk around the property, showing me the hydroelectric plant he'd built on a stream, and explaining what the land looked like before the lodge, which he had created in a place where once there had been nothing. I asked Bob what was the key to living such a great story, and Bob seemed uncomfortable with the idea he was anything special. But he wanted to answer my question, so he thought about it and said he didn't think we should be afraid to embrace whimsy. I asked him what he meant by *whimsy,* and he struggled to define it. He said it's that nagging idea that life could be magical; it could be special if we were only willing to take a few risks.

We spent nearly eight hours with the Goff family. They didn't want us to go, and we didn't want to go either. But around midnight we realized we still had to paddle several hours in order to make it to our campsite on the other side of the inlet, so we gathered our things on the dock.

I thanked Bob for the food and the towels and especially for the stories. I asked him if I could get in touch with him. He said he'd love to and gave me his e-mail address. I put my gear in the kayak, and Bob kneeled down on the wet dock and held it close as I lowered myself into the boat. I told him thanks and that I was sorry he got his knees wet. He looked at me and smiled and said it was nothing; just wait.

I wasn't sure what he meant by that, but as we pushed off the dock and the other guys got into their boats and pressed off, we back-paddled into the dark of the inlet, waving at the Goffs as they waved back at us. And then to our amazement, we saw all of them, fully dressed with shoes and jackets, take three steps together and jump into the water, coming up and waving and shouting their good-byes.

Part
Four

A Character Who Wants Something and Overcomes Conflict

twenty-five

A Better Story

I TOLD A FRIEND about having met my father and he listened with tears in his eyes. We were at a restaurant off the river, downtown, and he listened as though it were the most remarkable story he'd ever heard. I'd written a book about growing up without a father the previous year, and I also told my friend that I'd like to start a mentoring program of some sort through local churches, a program that could be replicated across the country. I wasn't very serious about it, it was just an idea, but my friend told me he knew the guy that could help. He said my story reminded him of a friend of his who lived in Portland, too, a man named Duncan Campbell. He told me I should get together with Duncan and tell him my idea. He gave me his number and I called and set up a meeting.

Duncan has a corner office in a skyscraper downtown. One window looks north toward Mt. St. Helens, down the Wilamette toward Steele Bridge and the Freemont Bridge, and the other looks east toward Mt. Hood and the Marquam Bridge, all the boats on the river hundreds of feet below winding up the Wilamette like toys. I hadn't realized when I set up the appointment that Duncan headed up a major timber investment firm that bore his name.

"I hear you're riding your bike across America," he said to me. Duncan has a round face like mine, he wears a sweater instead of a tie and his office is set up like a counselors office, two couches and a chair, pictures of his family behind his desk. He was warm and as inviting as a counselor, too. "Yes, I am. I said. I'm scared, but I'm going to give it a try."

"Are you going to start from Portland?" He asked.

"Los Angeles," I said. "Then Phoenix, New Mexico, Texas and so on before turning north toward Washington D.C."

"Wow," he laughed and smiled. "That's a long haul."

"Well, you know, I'll take it slow," I said, comforting myself I suppose.

"Are you going to be riding across east Texas?" He asked.

I believe so. I said.

"Well call me and tell me about that. Our firm just bought a large part of east Texas for a client, so I'm curious what you think of it when you ride across."

"Pardon me?" I said.

"Tell me what you think of it. I hear there are some hills. That will be tough biking, I suppose."

"You bought east Texas?" I clarified. "I didn't know east Texas was for sale."

"Oh sure, you know. A lot of timberland is for sale, Don. We'll harvest the trees and produce biomass. But you tell me what it's like. We have over a million acres out there, so I'm sure you'll be riding across our clients land."

"Ill do that," I said, secretly wondering how such a kind and unassuming man could have bought a chunk of Texas without having seen it personally.

"Hey, I hear you recently met your father." Duncan said, eager to change the subject off of business.

I told Duncan about the trip to Indiana and he shook his head as though to enjoy the adventure of it. He asked how I succeeded without a father, and I told him I had mentors along the way, guys from my church when I was a kid. Duncan asked about them, what kind of people they were, what sort of things they taught me. He could have listened to me talk about my mentors all day.

"I grew up over there," he said, pointing across the river into North Portland, one of the harder, more poverty stricken districts in Portland. His mother and father were both alcoholics, and Duncan said when he was a kid he used to walk the streets, knocking on the doors of bars hoping to find his parents.

"I raised myself," he said. "A lot of us did, in North Portland.

There weren't many parents around. We lived in a house, then a duplex, then an apartment until my mom moved into a single room. We were downwardly mobile," he said laughing. "I can't tell you how many times I sat in the car outside a bar," he continued, suddenly reflective. Duncan, even in his fifties, talked as though events in his distant history were as fresh as though they happened the previous week.

The most painful of Duncan's recollections was that he never had an adult friend, somebody to show him the way. There were teachers and coaches but nobody really focused on him specifically. Early on, though, Duncan became an exception to other children who were growing up in the neighborhood. He focused on his schoolwork, graduated from the University of Oregon, then continued there through law school, then worked in the juvenile justice system where he learned even more the need for kids to have mentors. Duncan left the juvenile justice system to become a lawyer, then started his timber investment corporation that succeeded dramatically.

"So I was sitting here in the office, Don, and one afternoon I looked across the river at the old neighborhood. I remembered sitting in my parents car waiting for them to come out of the bar, and I knew there was a kid somewhere down there sitting in a car. And I couldn't believe I'd forgotten. It hit me so hard. I had to do something."

"What did you do?" I asked.

"I resigned," he said. "Well," he clarified, "not exactly. But I started to resign. It takes a while. And I started a mentoring program called Friends for the Children. I hired a group of incredibly gifted mentors to befriend kids in elementary school. Each friend mentors eight kids, these kids are the worst problem kids in the school, the least of these, you know."

"That's incredible," I said.

"Did you know nearly 60% of the kids who start elementary school in low-income neighborhoods in Portland don't graduate from high school? But we graduate 85% of our kids. And they were the problem kids, remember. That's the power of a friend," Duncan said, smiling again.

It was suddenly an incredible honor to be in Duncan's office. An honor and an inspiration.

"So I hear you have an idea," He said.

"You know, Duncan, it doesn't feel like that big of a deal. I mean it's nothing like what you've done with Friends of the Children."

But I'd like to hear about it, Don.

I told him there are 27 million kids growing up without fathers, and there are 360,000 churches that could start small mentoring programs. They just needed somebody to resource and equip them.

Duncan patted the palm of his hand against the arm of his chair. He looked at the ceiling for a second and then smiled at me. "That's a great idea, Don. That is such a good idea."

To be honest, it had only been an idea. I mean I'd done

some serious thinking about it, but I wasn't sure whether it was a story I wanted to jump into. I wasn't sure it would work, and I certainly didn't feel qualified. I was afraid. But Duncan's story was inspirational. He convinced me that having grown up without a father and having had mentors who rescued me was enough to understand the issue. I could work around my liabilities with practice and time and the right people to help.

Later, after leaving his office, Duncan gave me a $25,000 check to seed the program. So I started an organization called The Mentoring Project. I hired a director and a small staff, and within the year we were mentoring eighty kids in Portland. I'd started an epic story of my own. And life no longer felt meaningless. It felt stressful and terrifying, but it definitely didn't feel meaningless.

twenty-six

The Thing About a Crossing

IT'S LIKE THIS when you live a story: The first part happens fast. You throw yourself into the narrative, and you're finally out in the water; the shore is pushing off behind you and the trees are getting smaller. The distant shore doesn't seem so far, and you can feel the resolution coming, the feeling of getting out of your boat and walking the distant beach. You think the thing is going to happen fast, that you'll paddle for a bit and arrive on the other side by lunch. But the truth is, it isn't going to be over soon.

The reward you get from a story is always less than you thought it would be, and the work is harder than you imagined. The point of a story is never about the ending, remember. It's about your character getting molded in the hard work of the middle. At some point the shore behind you stops getting smaller, and you paddle and wonder why the same strokes that used to move you now only rock the boat. You got the wife, but you don't know if you like her anymore and you've only been married five years. You want to wake up and walk into the living room in your underwear and watch football and let your daughters play with the dog because the far shore doesn't get closer no matter how hard you.

The shore you left is just as distant, and there is no going back; there is only the decision to paddle in place or stop, slide out of the hatch, and sink into the sea. Maybe there's another story at the bottom of the sea. Maybe you don't have to be in this story anymore.

It's been like this with all my crossings. I have a couple of boats and every couple of years I take them to Orcas Island and make the crossing from Orcas to Sucia, and it's always the same about leaving the shore so fast and getting to the middle and paddling in place for hours.

I knew it would be like that when we crossed the country on bikes too. I sent in my paperwork and did my miles in the mountains here in Oregon and showed up in Los Angeles, knowing we would start fast, that the Pacific would fade behind us and we'd be in Phoenix by sunset, and then we'd spend the life of Moses crossing Texas and the Delta—and it happened just as I thought it would. We grew into the roads, and the roads are where we lived. We slept in rock quarries and on the doorsteps of churches. I slept on the floor of a convenience store just off the caprock in Texas. I put my head by the beer to get some cold air, and it didn't matter that I had a condo back home or a bed, because you become the character in the story you are living, and whatever you were is gone. None of us thought the bike trip would end. We never felt that we were getting closer to the Atlantic Ocean. Even in Virginia, we felt as far as Louisiana.

The night we left Bob's dock, I didn't want to paddle through the night or across the wide inlet. We didn't leave his dock till after midnight, and we had to paddle for hours through the pitch black, and in the middle the inlet was so large and the dark was so dark we couldn't make out either shore. We had to guide ourselves by stars, each boat gliding close to another, just the sound of our oars coming in and out of the water to keep us close.

I think this is when most people give up on their stories. They come out of college wanting to change the world, wanting to get married, wanting to have kids and change the way people buy office supplies. But they get into the middle and discover it was harder than they thought. They can't see the distant shore anymore, and they wonder if their paddling is moving them forward. None of the trees behind them are getting smaller and none of the trees ahead are getting bigger. They take it out on their spouses, and they go looking for an easier story.

●　　●　　●

Robert McKee put down his coffee cup and leaned onto the podium. He put his hand on his forehead and wiped back his gray hair. He said, "You have to go there. You have to take your character to the place where he just can't take it anymore." He looked at us with a tenderness we hadn't seen in him before. "You've been there, haven't you? You've been out on the ledge. The marriage is over now; the dream is over now; nothing good can come from this."

He got louder. "Writing a story isn't about making your peaceful fantasies come true. The whole point of the story is the character arc. You didn't think joy could change a person, did you? Joy is what you feel when the conflict is over. But it's conflict that changes a person."

His voice was like thunder now. "You put your characters through hell. You put them through hell. That's the only way we change."

•   •   •

My friend Josh Shipp is one of the greatest communicators I've heard. He's only in his twenties but speaks around the country at high schools and is often a guest on MTV. Kids love him because he is funny and direct. Josh grew up in more than twenty foster homes, never knowing his real parents. And yet he is incredibly successful. I asked Josh why he's so healthy, so emotionally stable, considering his childhood. Josh told me something I'll never forget. He said, "Don, when something hard happens to you, you have two choices in how to deal with it. You can either get bitter, or better. I chose to get better. It's made all the difference."

•   •   •

If it weren't for the other guys in the kayak, I would have quit that night. We'd gotten up before sunrise, spent the day at Bob's, and were paddling now nearly twenty-four hours later. If it weren't for the other guys, I would have lay down in my hatch and slept and drifted out with the tide. But hours after I thought we'd arrive, I made out the gray wall of the cliff face on my right. We were close to it before we saw it, and it was like the walls of an ancient cathedral; our sounds were coming back at us off the rock. We had to follow the cliff to another, smaller crossing where there was a beach we'd made camp at on the way to the back of the inlet.

Then one of the guides pointed out bioluminescence was happening. He dropped his paddle into the water, and what looked like sparks splashed, and some of them floated like embers on top of the water. We all looked at our paddles and stirred them around in the water, and there in the darkness the ocean glowed. The farther we paddled into the opening, the darker the water got and the brighter the bioluminescence became. We could see each other now, because there were comet trails behind our boats, and there were sparks flying off our bows and onto our spray skirts, so bright you thought you needed to wipe them for fear they would burn the fabric.

It was four in the morning, but we were energized by the ocean. As we got closer to the other shore, there were a million fish swimming beneath our boats, each leaving a trail, and the ocean was flashing from beneath us as though fireworks were going off in the water. "I've never seen it like this," one of our guides said. He said he'd seen the ocean glow when you splashed your paddle, but he'd never seen the fish light up the water from underneath. When we were a hundred yards from shore and paddling into the lagoon, the whole ocean glowed like a swimming pool. None of us wanted to get out of our boats. I paddled around in circles in the lagoon, watching the fish streak beneath me like a meteor shower.

It's like this with every crossing, and with nearly every story too. You paddle until you no longer believe you can go any farther. And then suddenly, well after you thought it would happen, the other shore starts to grow, and it grows fast. The trees get taller and you can make out the crags in the cliffs, and then the shore reaches out to you, to welcome you home, almost pulling your boat onto the sand.

twenty-seven

The Pain Will Bind Us

I REMEMBER SEEING a story on *60 Minutes* about a group of American businessmen who were taken captive and held for ransom in South America. They were chained to each other for two years. They were kept in a cage and treated like dogs. In the interview, the three of them looked healthy, but I wondered about the scars they had on their bodies, the scars we couldn't see.

I noticed during the interview, the men were better with each other than most groups of men tend to be. They didn't finish each other's sentences, they knew when to stop talking and let the other express what he was better at expressing. And there was a love between them that was not a mushy love or even a brotherly love; it was a love I can only imagine being melded in the kind of torment that is only understood by somebody else experiencing the same pain. They were bound by conflict.

And it's not just big pain that binds. It's any sort of conflict. It's any sort of common purpose being arrived at through a tough middle that brings people together. There were fifteen of us who arrived in Los Angeles to ride our bikes across the country. We stayed in a little church in Santa Monica, sleeping on the floors and eating out of pizza boxes. None of us had known each other before the trip, and so we sat quietly around a large table and were briefed on our route and our routines and were warned about safety.

Aaron, the guy who ran the company that would guide us across the country, had lost his father in a bicycling accident the previous year, and so he kindly warned us to look out for each other, to call back approaching cars, and to warn each other about bad roads.

We would ride in the rain and perhaps some snow, in the hail and high winds, and we would ride from eight to fifteen hours a day until we got to our daily destination. "None of you is in the kind of shape to do this," Aaron said. "I don't mean that to be offensive. But it's going to be harder than you thought. But you will make it. Just don't stop, and stay together. You'll make it."

I don't think we would have chosen each other, the fifteen of us. I felt too old for the group. I was in my midthirties, and most of the group was at least ten years younger. There were a couple of people ten and twenty years older than me, but comparatively there weren't many of us old guys. I didn't know who to talk to or what to say. I hadn't seen the latest episode of *Saturday Night Live,* and so I didn't know the jokes. I felt out of place.

But we started pedaling, and none of that matters when you're riding bikes together. From the ocean, we weaved through the streets of Los Angeles, behind trucks and alongside buses, and we had to talk to each other about where the dangers were. And on the first day we climbed more than ten thousand feet into the mountains, and we were in such pain it no longer mattered how old we were or what we thought was cool or whether we knew who was in what band. We were just riding bikes, in a lot of pain, just glad there was somebody else who was crazy enough to sign up for the same mess.

•   •   •

I have a friend named Kaj who used to run an outdoor school in Canada. I went to visit him a couple of times, and each time I noticed he had a remarkable men's group at his school. The men tended to bond like brothers and respect each other and treat each other with dignity. I asked him once how he got the guys to bond like that, and Kaj said he believed the key to getting men to bond was to have them risk their lives together. I wasn't sure what he meant by that, so he explained he was talking about rock climbing and swift-water kayaking and that sort of thing. But one night I went to one of their men's events, and they didn't exactly sit around beating drums. Instead, they played capture the flag, but instead of flags they chucked little bottles of gasoline across fields into each other's campfires. The team whose campfire burned down last won. I honestly thought somebody was going to die. And then another night they made knights' outfits and rode bikes at each other with javelins made from long sticks with rolled up towels on the end. Only the towels had been dipped in gasoline and lit. I looked over at Kaj as though to say he was crazy, and he reminded me that men don't bond unless they risk their lives together, and that Canadians enjoy free health care.

After visiting Kaj, I realized how much of our lives are spent trying to avoid conflict. Half the commercials on television are selling us something that will make life easier. Part of me wonders if our stories aren't being stolen by the easy life.

I think it was about the third week on the bike trip when we began to bond. You'd think it would have been sooner, but you don't have a lot of time to talk about life when you're trying not to get hit by a car or when you're chewing on a lung because you're breathing so hard. But it was after Arizona, after we did 112 miles through 108-degree temperatures. It was after the mountains of New Mexico and those hot, wet hills of Texas. It was after we slept under an overpass, and after one of us fell and broke her tailbone. It slowly happened in our sub-conscious that though we were different, there was nobody else having these experiences with us. It was just us. We'd call and talk to the people back home about it, but all we could do was say some words about how hot it was or how much our legs hurt. But when we said those words to each other, each of us had a mental catalog of similar experiences, and those experiences bound us together.

I saw a documentary once about a group of families who transplanted from their suburban lives into rural Montana, where they lived on the open prairie for a solid year. Each family had to build their own cabin and live off the land. The family I remember most had come from the coast of California where they had a multimillion-dollar mansion on a cliff over-looking the ocean. The father had signed the family up for the adventure because his marriage wasn't doing well, and the conflict was affecting the kids. And so, they went from a thirty-room mansion to a single room in a field, without elec-tricity, without running water. There was a father and mother and two teenagers, a son and a daughter. The men had to work the field, even though neither father nor son had any experi-ence in farming. And the girls spent what seemed like all day preparing food for three simple meals. But the interesting thing is that they bonded. Without all the trappings of mod-ern life, and without the gadgets we use to make life simple, the family came together.

I was saddened at the end of the documentary when, after a year, the filmmakers went back to visit each family. They interviewed the young girl who was sitting in the hot tub behind the mansion, looking down over the beach. The interviewer asked if she was glad to be home. And the girl sat and thought for a moment and then said no. She said her mother and father were fighting again, and she never saw her brother. There was a tear coming down her cheek as she said this. She said she wished they could go back to Montana where everything was easier.

The day I remember most while crossing the country was the day we rode through Joshua Tree. I got away from the group by perhaps thirty miles, and as the temperature broke a hundred degrees, I was forced to look for shade. The heat was coming up off the pavement like an oven. But there were no trees. After ten more miles, I found a metal shed next to a railroad track, and about six inches of shade landing on some concrete next to the shed. I laid my body down and put my head in the shade where there was a hot breeze swirling around. I just needed a break from the sun. I knew I had fifty more miles to go, and the miles would be, perhaps, the most miserable of my life. But in that place, I remembered about story, about how every conflict, no matter how hard, comes back to bless the protagonist if he will face his fate with courage. There is no conflict man can endure that will not produce a blessing. And I smiled. I'm not saying I was happy, but for some reason I smiled. *It hurts now, but I'll love this memory,* I thought to myself. And I do.

twenty-eight

A Tree in a Story About a Forest

THE GIRL I went to Peru with and I dated for a while. We even talked about getting married. We looked for a church, and we planned our home—we would knock down a wall in my guest bedroom so we could each have an office. We named our kids. And all that was something new to me. Not the dating, but the marriage part. I'm an idealist by nature, and though I'd been in a few long-term relationships, I knew I didn't have the money to get married; so I never said "I love you," and I never thought about renting a tuxedo.

Because of this, my previous relationships had ended in a directionless fog that women, God bless them, can't seem to endure. They all want to go to the moon. But this girl was different. And not only was she different; I was in a different place when we started dating. I could afford a family if I wanted, and I was in that midthirty range, where people stop talking about relationships because they assume you have issues.

So I met a girl, and we fell in love, and I knew, in that knowing beyond all knowing that kids in high school talk about, she was the one. When I was on that kayaking trip, I sat on a beach and wrote a letter, and for the first time said, "I love you" to a woman. I knew when I wrote those words, I was *in*, that I would marry her in a church and there would be a cake and an open bar and some dancing. I wasn't scared either, like people are scared when they have issues. I ordered a ring, and we started premarital counseling and enjoyed the natural high the body creates to trick us into thinking another human being might rescue us, something I now believe is a lie that ends many marriages.

If you ask me, we make too much of worldly love. I like it as a metaphor, but making too much of love is like trying not to be where a tree falls in the forest so you can hear it. It's like chasing a leprechaun.

In the end, my girlfriend and I put too much pressure on each other because we both thought the other person was Jesus. I think of it as nearly trivial now, but when those experiences are happening, they are monuments; you walk around in the emotions like Texans on their first trip to the Rockies.

We were both passionate and strong-willed people, and this became our undoing. I won't go into details, because they are the same as a million other romantic disasters. Essentially, though, it felt like the Tower of Babel had been planted between us, because for no lack of effort, once we started arguing, we could no longer communicate our basic needs. Each failed attempt to talk things out became a wall between us, skin thick, so every conversation had the resonance of talking to yourself. What was once passion turned into anger, and anger turned into resentment, and in a toxic swamp of hurt feelings, we broke up on a return flight from a place we had gone so our families could meet.

I remember landing in Portland and feeling that, even as the wheels hit the runway, my soul was collecting fluid. We sat next to each other in tears as other passengers stole glances. We took a cab back to my house and sat silently in the backseat, both of us hoping the other might suddenly resurrect from the dead. In the days that followed, the wall got wider and the conversations grew shorter until we were only grunting the way people must have done when they lived in caves.

My life got dark. As the weeks went on, I would stand at the window in my condo and look down at the trees lining up toward the mountain, and I couldn't remember why I once thought of those trees as congregants singing hymns toward an altar.

You never see this in movies. Characters don't look at themselves in the bathroom mirror for hours wondering why they can no longer feel. Characters in movies progress.

But I didn't know what direction to move. I was walking down Thirteenth Street and caught my reflection in the window of the Ugly Mug. I stood for an embarrassingly long time wondering how the lines around my eyes had suddenly grown so deep. There was a woman sitting at the counter using a laptop who stared back at me long enough to wake me from my trance, so I kept walking down the street, remembering the time my girlfriend had sat gangly and laughing in the red wagon I own, something the previous owner of my condo left when they moved their furniture out. I used to pull her in the wagon down that street and through the aisles of the market on Tacoma. People would watch us as I rolled her down the aisle and she grabbed the ingredients off the shelf we needed for dinner, calling out produce, then pasta, then cheese.

I didn't shave. I didn't eat. As my story stopped, so did I. You can't go on without a story any longer than you can read a book about nothing.

It's remarkable to me how a room or a street or other characters only make sense in the context of a story. Without a personal narrative, even something as basic as my furniture seemed like a rambling description of brown leather and wooden legs flung off the pen of an amateur novelist.

After a tragedy, I think God gives us a period of numbing as a kind of grace. Perhaps he knows our small minds, given so easily to false hope, couldn't handle the full brunt of reality. My anesthetized state reminded me of the time I broke my wrist in a biking accident. I had gone over a ledge and got the wind knocked out of me when I hit the ground. By the time my friends found me, I was sitting cross-legged in the leaves studying the broken bones that were making contortions under my skin. I kept wondering why it didn't hurt. I wondered that for hours, till late that night when my roommate rushed me to the emergency room while I sat next to him in the passenger's seat, holding my wrist tightly against my lap, pressing my head against the dashboard.

After the breakup, I sat around the house on my useless furniture rubbing my hand across my heart, wondering when I was going to feel the fracture in my chest.

Not too much later, the girl moved to Switzerland. The guy at the jewelry store kept leaving animated messages on my voice mail saying the ring was ready and wondering out loud how excited she would be when I got down on one knee. I wondered why the messages didn't mean anything to me, and I started to believe I was selfish and incapable of feeling. Even though I'd paid for most of the ring, I never returned the jeweler's calls.

What I did, instead, was throw myself into my work, trying to restart my story as though the previous pages hadn't happened. I flew around delivering speeches, playing a part like an actor. I talked about meaning and fulfillment and how a good ambition is the path to living a meaningful life. It was all very clean and neat on the outside, but on the inside my narrative was incoherent.

But all that ended at a conference in Los Angeles where I was scheduled to give a speech. I was only there for a few hours, but I asked for a hotel room to shower and go over my notes. I had a yellow pad in front of me and was scribbling an outline and the television was on a football game when it occurred to me I was thirty-six and unable to navigate a serious relationship. I knew then the shock was wearing off. A certain fear grew. *They don't have an emergency room for the kind of pain that is about to happen to me*, I thought.

I put my pen down on the bed and waited. Then another thought came that said I would be living the rest of my life alone because I was unlovable. The thought I could no longer eat or drink would have been less devastating. I sat in a haze for a minute and was startled when the yellow pad slipped off my knee onto the floor. The bones in my chest turned their sharp ends outward and made a tent of the skin over my heart. I told myself it wasn't true, that I was a perfectly good person and God could change whatever it was that made me contemptible. I told myself there was still time. But counselors from hell spoke to me from under the pillows and behind the chairs until they had the big voice.

Before this, I couldn't understand why a person would commit suicide. And while I now have the perspective that only comes from distance, and the perspective always comes, I know the power a lie has to shrink time into what seems the eternal end of things. It is a true miracle I survived that hour. I wasn't numb anymore. I was allowed to feel the brunt of it. The bones penetrated my chest in a sudden rip, emptying a body of blood down my shirt and onto my lap. The blood pooled in the lap of my pants and seeped into the carpet in my hotel room. I clasped my hand over my heart and knelt between the bed and the television and rolled onto the floor and cried out to God a lamenting demand that he would come and save me from the sorrow that, for the immensity of it, I could only attribute to him in the first place. I didn't want to learn whatever it was he wanted to teach me. I cried out to him an angry petition for rescue. I doubted him and needed him at the same time. God seemed to me, in that moment, a cruel father burning a scar into my skin with his cigarette. And yet I knew he was the only one with the power to make the pain go away.

●　　●　　●

I recently read the biography of Victor Frankl, an Austrian neurologist and psychologist who in 1942 was deported to Theresienstadt, a Nazi concentration camp that housed Jews in transit to Auschwitz. While in the camp, and later in Auschwitz, Frankl studied and journaled about his and others' conditions of despondency. He was separated from his wife and lost his parents in the ghetto, yet he still worked to prevent suicide among his fellow prisoners. Interfering with suicides was prohibited by Nazi guards, but Frankl whispered in people's ears all the same. The essence of his whispers were that life, even amid the absurdity of human suffering, still had meaning. Suffering, as absurd as it seemed, pointed to a greater story in which, if one would only construe himself as a character within, he could find fulfillment in his tragic role, knowing the plot was heading toward redemption. Such an understanding would take immense humility and immeasurable faith, a perspective perhaps achieved only in the context of near hopelessness.

Frankl's papers, written after surviving the camps, and even after losing his wife to the Nazis, indicated a philosophical conclusion that misery, though seemingly ridiculous, indicates life itself has the potential of meaning, and therefore pain itself must also have meaning. Contrary to Freud's posit that man's greatest pursuit is of pleasure, Frankl argued life is a pursuit of meaning itself, and that search for meaning provides the basis for a person's motivation. Pain then, if one could have faith in something greater than himself, might be a path to experiencing a meaning beyond the false gratification of personal comfort.

For the prisoners Frankl helped in the concentration camps, a chance for survival was increased by a person's ability to dwell in a spiritual domain, a place where the SS could not intrude. In essence, the prisoners whom Frankl influenced were convinced to surrender their tragic experiences to the greater whole of a grander epic, and in that role they found a purpose to continue living.

●　●　●

The oldest book of the Bible is supposedly the book of Job. It is a book about suffering, and it reads as though God is saying to the world, *Before we get started, there's this one thing I have to tell you. Things are going to get bad.*

Job is a good man whom God allows to be destroyed, except for his life. God allows Job's family to be taken, along with his wealth and his health. Job calls out to God, asking why God would let this happen.

God does not answer Job's question. It's as though God starts off his message to the world by explaining there are painful realities in life we cannot and will never understand. Instead, he appears to Job in a whirlwind and asks if Job knows who stops the waves on the shore or stores the snow in Wichita every winter. He asks Job who manages the constellations that reel through the night sky.

And that is essentially all God says to Job. God doesn't explain pain philosophically or even list its benefits. God says to Job, *Job, I know what I am doing, and this whole thing isn't about you.*

Job responds, even before his health and wealth are restored by saying, "All of this is too wonderful for me." Job found contentment and even joy, outside the context of comfort, health or stability. He inderstood the story was not about him, and he cared more about the story than he did about himself.

● ● ●

But the world was not too wonderful for me back in Los Angeles. Nonetheless, I gathered myself enough to go down and give the speech. I don't remember what I said, but I remember people laughing and nodding, and when I was done, the pain came back, and I stood and talked to people and watched their mouths move, but I didn't know what they were saying.

That night I flew a red-eye to Nashville where I was going to attend a friend's wedding. There wasn't anybody in the seat next to me, so I ordered a drink and laid back and imagined Victor Frankl. I remembered him in the concentration camp, and I imagined him whispering in my ear. I didn't want to hear him at first. I didn't want to get well, because if I got well, nobody would come and save me anymore. And I didn't want to get well, because while I could not control my happiness, I could control my misery, and I would rather have had control than live in the tension of *what if*. A chance of hope is no pacifier against a sure tragedy.

But Victor Frankl whispered in my ear all the same. He said to me I was a tree in a story about a forest, and that it was arrogant of me to believe any differently. And he told me the story of the forest is better than the story of the tree.

●　　●　　●

The wedding in Nashville was a wedding in the round, so through and around James and Jena you could see the rest of the crowd. On all sides there were old friends who'd had children since I last saw them, or who had divorced, or who had also gotten married. We sat in silence and creaked in our chairs as James and Jena recited their vows, and our minds went up like high branches over them and over each other.

The next night, I was back at my friend Jim's. I sat on his deck and made a fire. I sat and watched deer cross the driveway that climbs through a hundred trees up to his house, and because it was winter I could see through the skeletal limbs the lights of distant neighborhoods clustered together as though for warmth. And at one point I turned when I heard a tree drop a heavy limb to the ground. I sat by the fire until the sun came up; and asked God to help me understand the story of the forest and what it meant to be a tree in that story.

twenty-nine

The Reason God Hasn't Fixed You Yet

I'M CONVINCED THE most fantastical moment in story, the point when all the tension is finally relieved, doesn't actually happen in real life. And I mean that seriously. I've thought about it fifty different ways, but I can't figure out how a human life actually climaxes so that everything on the other side of a particular moment is made to be okay. It happens all the time in movies and books, but it won't happen to me—and I'm sorry to say, it won't happen to you either.

Maybe the reason we like stories so much is because they deliver wish fulfillment. Maybe we sit in the dark and shovel sugar into our mouths because in so many stories everything is made right, and we secretly long for that ourselves.

It was touching when Steve, Ben, and I realized what the climax to our movie was going to be. We'd been writing toward it for more than a year, and we were practically in tears when we finally wrote that part of the script. It was a scene in which two characters met in confrontation, and one asked the other for forgiveness. We were back at Jim's house in Tennessee, sitting around his table. I was saying the words my character needed to say, Ben was adding dialogue from the other character, and Steve was typing it in as fast as he could. Neither Ben nor I were looking at each other, because if we did we'd have cried—we'd have cried over characters who didn't exist resolving a tension that never really happened. There's just something in the DNA of a human that responds to the idea of an event, a moment in which the upheaval we've all been working around is finally laid to rest.

But regardless how passionate the utopianists are, I simply don't believe utopia is going to happen. I don't believe we are going to be rescued. I don't believe an act of man will make things on earth perfect, and I don't believe God will intervene before I die, or for that matter before you die. I believe, instead, we will go on longing for a resolution that will not come, not within life as we know it, anyway.

If you think about it, an enormous amount of damage is created by the myth of utopia. There is an intrinsic feeling in nearly every person that your life could be perfect if you only had such-and-such a car or such-and-such a spouse or such-and-such a job. We believe we will be made whole by our accomplishments, our possessions, or our social status. It's written in the fabric of our DNA that life used to be beautiful and now it isn't, and if only this and if only that, it would be beautiful again.

I saw a story on *60 Minutes* a few months ago about the happiest country in the world. It was Denmark. A study done by a British university ranked the happiest countries, and America was far down the list, but Denmark was on top. Morley Safer explored why. Ruling out financial status, physical health, and even social freedom, he landed on a single characteristic of the Danes that allowed them such contentment. The reason Danes are so happy was this: they had low expectations.

I'm not making that up. There is something in Denmark's culture that allows them to look at life realistically. They don't expect products to fulfill them or relationships to end all their problems. In fact, in the final interview of the segment, Safer was sitting across from a Danish man and remarked to him that when Americans find out the happiest place on earth is Denmark, they are going to want to move there. Without missing a beat, the Danish man looked at Morley and said, "Well, honestly, they will probably be let down."

I don't mean to insinuate there are no minor climaxes to human stories. There are. A kid can try to make the football team and in a moment of climax see his name on the coach's list. A girl can want to get married and feel euphoric when the man of her dreams slides a ring on her finger. But these aren't the stories I'm talking about. These are substories. When that kid makes the football team, he is going to find out that playing football is hard, and he's going to find himself in the middle of yet another story. And the girl is going to wake up three months into her marriage and realize she is, in fact, still lonely, and so many of her issues haven't gone away. And if both of these people aren't careful, they're going to get depressed because they thought the climax to their substory was actually a climax to the human story, and it wasn't. The human story goes on.

Growing up in church, we were taught that Jesus was the answer to all our problems. We were taught that there was a circle-shaped hole in our heart and that we had tried to fill it with the square pegs of sex, drugs, and rock and roll; but only the circle peg of Jesus could fill our hole. I became a Christian based, in part, on this promise, but the hole never really went away. To be sure, I like Jesus, and I still follow him, but the idea that Jesus will make everything better is a lie. It's basically biblical theology translated into the language of infomercials. The truth is, the apostles never really promise Jesus is going to make everything better here on earth. Can you imagine an info-mercial with Paul, testifying to the amazing product of Jesus, saying that he once had power and authority, and since he tried Jesus he's been moved from prison to prison, beaten, and rou-tinely bitten by snakes? I don't think many people would be buying that product. Peter couldn't do any better. He was cruci-fied upside down, by some reports. Stephen was stoned outside the city gates. John, supposedly, was boiled in oil. It's hard to imagine how a religion steeped in so much pain and sacrifice turned into a promise for earthly euphoria. I think Jesus can make things better, but I don't think he is going to make things perfect. Not here, and not now.

What I love about the true gospel of Jesus, though, is that it offers hope. Paul has hope our souls will be made complete. It will happen in heaven, where there will be a wedding and a feast. I wonder if that's why so many happy stories end in weddings and feasts. Paul says Jesus is the hope that will not disappoint. I find that comforting. That helps me get through the day, to be honest. It even makes me content somehow. Maybe that's what Paul meant when he said he'd learned the secret of contentment.

After the girl I'd dated had been in Switzerland for a while, and as I continued to see a counselor, I realized that for years I'd thought of love as something that would complete me, make all my troubles go away. I worshipped at the altar of romantic completion. And it had cost me, plenty of times. And it had cost most of the girls I'd dated, too, because I wanted them to be something they couldn't be. It's too much pressure to put on a person. I think that's why so many couples fight, because they want their partners to validate them and affirm them, and if they don't get that, they feel as though they're going to die. And so they lash out. But it's a terrible thing to wake up and realize the person you just finished crucifying didn't turn out to be Jesus.

I was interviewing my friend Susan Isaacs after her book *Angry Conversations with God* came out. We were in front of a live audience, and I was reading questions to her off of index cards submitted by the audience. Because so much of her book talks about relational needs, relational fulfillment and unful-fillment, one of the questions asked was whether she believed there was one true love for every person.

Susan essentially said no. And she said that with her husband sitting right there in the audience. She said she and her husband believed they were a cherished prize for each other, and they would probably drive any other people mad. But then she said something I thought was wise. She said she had married a guy, and he was just a guy. He wasn't going to make all her problems go away, because he was just a guy. And that freed her to really love him as a guy, not as an ultimate problem solver. And because her husband believed she was just a girl, he was free to really love her too. Neither needed the other to make everything okay. They were simply content to have good company through life's conflicts. I thought that was beautiful.

There is a lot of money and power to be had in convincing people we can create an Eden here on earth. Cults are formed when leaders make such absurd promises. Products are sold convincing people that they are missing out on the perfect life. And political groups tend to scare people by convincing them we are losing Eden, or inspire people by telling them we can rebuild what God has destroyed. We all get worked into a frenzy over things that will not happen until Jesus returns. The truth is, we can make things a little better or a little worse, but utopia doesn't hang in the balance of our vote or of what products we buy.

All of this may sound depressing to you, but I don't mean it to be. I've lived some good stories now, and those stories have improved the quality of my life. But I've also let go of the idea things will ever be made perfect, at least while I am walking around on this planet. I've let go of the idea that this life has a climax. I'm trying to be more Danish, I guess. And the thing is, it works. When you stop expecting people to be perfect, you can like them for who they are. And when you stop expecting material possessions to complete you, you'd be surprised at how much pleasure you get in material possessions. And when you stop expecting God to end all your troubles, you'd be surprised how much you like spending time with God.

Do I still think there will be a day when all wrongs are made right, when our souls find the completion they are looking for? I do. But when all things are made right, it won't be because of some preacher or snake-oil salesman or politician or writer making promises in his book. I think, instead, this will be done by Jesus. And it will be at a wedding. And there will be a feast.

thirty

Great Stories Have Memorable Scenes

MY FRIEND MEGAN told me when she was a kid she went to a summer camp based on the promise it would be the most memorable week of her life. She's older now but told me the camp lived up to its promise. When I asked why the camp was so great, she didn't tell me that it was *fun* or she met *great people*, although those things were true. Instead, she told me about *scenes*. She described an obstacle course in which she and her friends had to crawl through knee-deep mud and that she went parasailing on a lake at sunset. She described the roof of her cabin, upon which she and her friends climbed to talk about boys until the sun came up. It had been nearly fifteen years since that camp, but when she talked about it, she got so excited she had to stand up.

When Steve, Ben, and I were writing the screenplay, I suggested our characters go to a coffee shop to hash out, in conversation, a bit of the conflict. But Ben and Steve told me that sort of scene isn't memorable, and it was time for the plot of the story to unfold in a more memorable way. I didn't know exactly what they meant, but I started noticing, in movies, scenes often take place in strange places. There was the scene in *Good Will Hunting* where Will and his friend have a conversation at a batting cage, except Will is in the middle of the cage, throwing pitches. And there's the scene in *Garden State* where the characters are standing in the rain on the edge of a cliff right next to a guy's house that was made from a boat. And even in *Rocky*, they take his training into a meat locker so he can punch giant slabs of beef.

This idea is true in life too. I had a friend in town for six weeks this year. She was visiting Oregon and doing some work here, and over the six weeks we rented some movies and went to coffee and ate at a few restaurants. We had great conversations. But honestly, when I think back on those six weeks, what I really remember are the few times when we made an extra effort to do something memorable. We took my dog Lucy for a hike and introduced her to her first waterfall. We took the kayaks out on the river and strapped them together to have a floating picnic. When we look back on our lives, what we will remember are the crazy things we did, the times we worked harder to make a day stand out.

I was thinking about what Steve and Ben said about memorable scenes when some friends and I were coming back from a hike at Silver Falls. We were driving through the foothills of the Cascades, and in the evening light, the fields were sloping out like brush strokes. I wasn't noticing the hills around us at first, because I was tired and ready to get home, but then I started seeing how red the fields were, and then my friend Joy said something about it, and then Kacie agreed that the light was getting beautiful. One of my favorite scenes in a movie is from Wes Anderson's *Bottle Rocket*, in which Dignan is standing in a field shooting a Roman candle at the ground and Anthony walks in slowly from the distance. I won't get into what the scene is about, but I do know the peculiar image of an open field and a guy shooting a Roman candle at the ground has stayed in my mind like a painting. When we were driving through the fields that night, I was thinking about that scene, too, and then Joy mentioned she used to love running through open fields when she was a little girl. Before I started thinking of life as a story, I wouldn't have thought much of a comment like that. But the new me figured it out in a hurry. Good stories contain memorable scenes, Steve and Ben would say.

When we came to the next field, I pulled the truck over, and the girls giggled like they were in high school or something. We all got out, and Joy ran across the street and into the field until she became a speck on the horizon. The rest of us walked partway up a hill, and Joy came back and joined us in time to see the sun drop beneath the coastal range. And from behind us the darker blue came out of the mountains like music.

When we were walking back, I noticed the hill behind us was silhouetting, and I wondered how fun it would be to drive the truck to the top. When we got back in the truck, I drove across the road and through the ditch and gunned it to the top of the hill. It felt like we were on a roller coaster; it felt dangerous and wrong and so good. At the top we got out and stood on the hill and watched the last bit of light run off the hills, like rainwater into the Pacific.

●   ●   ●

My friend Randy recently created a great memory with his daughter. When his daughter entered high school, she started to get more interested in girl things, and the two of them didn't talk as much as they used to. When she got asked to the prom, she was very excited. Her dad simply responded by saying congratulations. She quickly slid past him and jumped up and down in front of her mom. He didn't mean to be dismissive, but he didn't know what he was supposed to say.

About a week later he was watching *SportsCenter* when his wife and daughter came home with a dress. They didn't say anything to him, knowing he wouldn't be interested, and went back to the daughter's bedroom so she could put it on. When she came into the living room to show her dad, he turned down the volume and told her she looked nice, that it was a nice color, but when she curtsied and thanked him and walked away he knew he should have said more. He wanted to tell her that she was beautiful and that she was his princess and all the stuff fathers find so hard to say to their daughters. He turned the television back on and tried to pay attention to the scores, but all of this kept bugging him. Then he came up with an idea. He decided to create a memorable scene, if you will. He turned off the television and went into his closet and put on his suit. Without letting his wife or daughter see him, he found the family camera and knocked on her door. When his daughter opened the door, she was still in the dress and her mother was sitting on the bed with stick-pins in her mouth. My friend said his wife almost swallowed the pins.

"Honey," my friend said to his wife, "would you mind taking a picture of us?"

"Daddy, you're wearing a suit," his daughter said, confused.

"I want to look good in the picture too," he told her.

The three of them ended up dancing in the living room until one in the morning, my friend and his wife telling stories about their own prom dates and how they wished they would have known each other in high school.

●　❋　●

When I heard this story, I remembered Bob and his family jumping off the dock at the lodge. For no good reason, they jumped into the water fully clothed, just so they could say good-bye to us in a way that cost them something, that branded a scene into our minds that we could remember for years to come. A good movie has memorable scenes, and so does a good life.

•   •   •

I recently encountered an exceptional movie called *Darius Goes West*. It's a documentary that, while it never had a wide release, won a handful of awards at various festivals. The story of the documentary follows a group of friends, one of whom has muscular dystrophy and slowly loses mobility. Darius is fifteen years old and has already lost a brother to MS. After realizing Darius had never left his hometown of Athens, Georgia, his friends raised money to take him to California, where they hoped MTV would "pimp" Darius's wheelchair.

What unfolds in the film is a series of memorable scenes. They stay at a five-star hotel in New Orleans and then take their friend on a swamp-boat ride. The group celebrates the fifteenth anniversary of the Americans with Disabilities Act in an enormous cavern in New Mexico. They plant Darius in the middle of a raft and take him down the Colorado River. They stay up all night in the desert, counting shooting stars, and the next morning they wheel Darius to the edge of the Grand Canyon, where he sits speechless until his eyes well up with tears. When they finally get to California, they take Darius on a hot air-balloon ride above Napa Valley, and he sits low in the basket stretching his neck to see more of the view, wearing a smile I've only seen brighter on newborn babies discovering color and feeling. The most memorable scene of the film, I think, has the guys rolling Darius's wheelchair into the ocean, removing him from his chair, and holding him as the waves crash over his body. Darius feels his feet hit the ocean floor and realizes, for the first time in years, he is standing. He laughs uncontrollably as his friends hold him under his arms so that his feet dangle and scrape against the sand.

What I love most about that film is that it wasn't fiction; it was real people creating real moments, really bonding through insanely beautiful experiences.

Darius Goes West is more than a memorable film; it is the story of a group of friends who intentionally create a memorable life.

I don't think memorable scenes help a story make sense. Other principles accomplish that. What memorable scenes do is punctuate the existing rise and fall of a narrative. The ambition of getting Darius a better wheelchair had the makings of a terrific story, but it's the way in which they got there that I will never forget. And neither will Darius.

•   ✦   •

I like those scenes in the Bible where God stops people and asks them to build an altar. You'd think He was making them do that for Himself, but I don't think God really gets much from looking at a pile of rocks. Instead, I think God wanted his people to build altars for their sake, something that would help them remember, something they could look back on and remember the time when they were rescued, or they were given grace.

After studying memorable scenes, I realized why it was Bob and his family jump into the inlet when people are leaving the lodge. It's a memory. It's a way that they, and also their guests, will never forget their visit.

But it's like I said before, about writers not really wanting to write. We have to force ourselves to create these scenes. We have to get up off the couch and turn the television off, we have to blow up the inner-tubes and head to the river. We have to write the poem and deliver it in person. We have to pull the car off the road and hike to the top of the hill. We have to put on our suits, we have to dance at weddings. We have to make altars.

Part
Five

A Character Who
Wants Something
and Overcomes
Conflict to Get It

thirty-one

Squeezing the Cat

LIKE I SAID, I was one of the oldest guys on the bike trip. But I wasn't the oldest. The oldest was a guy named Mike Barrow, who was in his midfifties, and who proved to be an inspiration to the rest of us. We gave him the nickname Iron Mike, because he wouldn't quit. He hunched over his bike and worked his legs like slow pistons on a steam train that was digging through the mountains of New Mexico and the balmy July heat of Louisiana. Mike was, for all of us, one of the most pleasant people to ride alongside, always bringing up some story from his Navy days or reaching into his bag to hand us a Snickers bar as he passed, instructing us to eat some calories because we'll need them if we are going to catch the old man.

On a night in Texas we were all staying in a farm house

we'd rented and some boy asked Mike to tell his story. I confess I thought I already knew much of what there was to know about Mike, that he was a colorful man with the resolve of a machine. But, and perhaps because he was old enough not to care what anybody thought about him, Mike told us a lot more about himself, and what we didn't know was rather surprising.

Mike was on his fourth marriage, and his previous marriages had failed because of a lack of discipline and resolve. Mike had been a nurse and became addicted to drugs and that addiction affected most of his decisions. He got choked up when he told us that once he stole drugs from a patient he was caring for, giving the patient less than what was needed to numb their pain. He abandoned his wife and their children. He even had a kid out there he'd never met. "I've never done anything right," he said to us. "This whole right living thing is fairly new to me. I was a mess. I mean a real mess."

One of the darker scenes in Mike's story, and perhaps one of the more amusing, depending on how you look at it, was when Mike began an affair with a woman he worked with at the hospital. She was nearly half his age, and he was still using drugs, and when the woman told him she didn't want to see him anymore, he went to her house while she wasn't there and kidnapped her cat. He then called her on the phone and told her she had to see him, or he'd hurt the cat. He put the phone on the floor and squeezed the cat into the phone until it whined, then picked up the phone again to hear her response. The woman called the police and Mike was arrested.

But not all the scenes in Mike's life had been so depravingly charming. We all got quiet when Mike started talking about his childhood. He held back tears when he talked about the day his father killed himself. And he didn't hold them back when he talked about the day he got into the bathtub and slit his wrist, his nearly dead body found by his brother.

"It was years ago, you know." Mike said. "I've changed. God helped me change."

We'd all gone on the ride for different reasons. I signed up because I wanted a practice story, an adventure. Other motivations were more pure, to raise money and awareness for the people of Africa. But for all the good reasons for going on the ride, Mike's was my favorite.

There on the big covered porch of the farm house in Texas, after a grueling day riding in a sun only hotter on Mars, when we were all wishing we didn't have to get up and do it again the next day, Mike told us the reason he signed up to ride across America. He said he signed up so he could finish. He said he'd quit three marriages, and he wouldn't quit a fourth. He said he'd quit on children, and he didn't want to quit on the responsibility of being a father with the ones who still loved him. He started crying, then. Mike said he knew deep down he'd changed. "I'm going to finish this thing," Mike said. "I'm not a quitter anymore."

thirty-two

The Beauty of a Tragedy

MY FRIEND JIM lost his wife of twenty-seven years this fall. She was a terrific and deliberate woman. I met them just after she found out she had cancer, when four of us went out to dinner at a restaurant in Indiana, she and three men. We all ordered chicken, and she ordered steak. She sat small behind her plate and cut through the meat braggingly.

Jim has a company that books speakers and had taken me on as a client. He is a terrific businessman and very organized, and once I signed with him, the disorganization that had caused so much stress in my life went away. At the time I felt I was carrying a thousand pounds up a mountain when Jim came beside me and carried it on his shoulders like a sack of feathers. He did this while he was carrying his marriage and the weight of their two grown sons, all of them tangled up in Janice's cancer.

One afternoon we were sitting in the chairs under the tree in my front yard when I asked how Janice was doing. He gave me a formal report about new medicines and treatments, and then his eyes welled up and he got quiet. The truth is, she wasn't doing well.

Not long after Jim returned to Nashville, he sent an update saying that Janice was back in the hospital and losing weight. The doctors had tried every known strategy and had explained to Jim that Janice's days were few. The tone of Jim's e-mail update was subdued and reflective. He didn't really know how to process the idea of losing his wife.

•   •   •

The following month I was speaking in Boston, and Jim met me there because his sons were living in the city. Janice was seventy pounds then and spending most of her days in bed, being cared for by Jim, friends, and a nurse. In Boston Jim spent the day with the boys. They talked about their mother, and he prepared them for the inevitable. One of the boys was in a band, and that night Jim went to one of his concerts. The show was held in a tiny basement where a hundred college students crammed shoulder to shoulder and smoked cigarettes, spilled glasses of cheap beer, and bobbed their heads to his son's band.

The next night Jim stayed up late in my hotel room and drank a bottle of wine, and he told me how old and tall he felt at the concert. He laughed when he described the endless line of guys peeing off the deck under which they would occasionally stand to get air.

We drank more wine and got solemn, and Jim wondered out loud whether the boys were ready. I told him they couldn't possibly be ready. He agreed. I asked him if *he* was ready, and part of me wanted to tell him that after Janice died, he should sell the house and get a condo and join a gym and change everything in a hurry so he wouldn't have to deal with the pain. I didn't say these things, and I'm glad I didn't, because those are the things people who have never been married say. He said another friend had recommended he not change anything after her passing, that he should live in the house and grieve and say good-bye for as long as it might take. That seemed true to me, as soon as he said it, and I knew at once there was an entire part of the human experience I didn't understand.

"But all of that is to come," Jim said. "She is still here. We have her, for now." Jim drank the last of the glass of wine and filled it again. He took another sip and set the glass on the table next to us. He breathed deep and then told me how hard it was to watch her slip in and out of consciousness and how much he cherished the hour or two each day when she had the strength to talk. He would sit in the chair by her bed and watch as her eyes began to stir. He would pray she could hear and talk that day, if only for a few minutes, that he could say anything to her and she would understand the words and say something back.

Anybody who knows Jim likes him very much, but it was in that conversation, when the infinitely deep well of love the man had within himself was revealed, that he became more than a partner in projects to me, more than a friend, even. I hated that it took pain to open the curtain revealing the man's heart, but it did and it does. We don't know how much we are capable of loving until the people we love are being taken away, until a beautiful story is ending. The hotel room I was in was high and looked down on Boston. I glanced over and thought about all the people in that city and knew, perhaps, the most human of human beings within twenty miles was sitting across from me.

●　　●　　●

It was nearly midnight when Jim left my hotel room in Boston. We hugged and said good night. When he left I looked down on the Charles River and the steaming buildings and the ice on the bridges; then I closed the curtains and went to bed. When I woke in the morning and called him for breakfast, he was gone. In the hallway outside my room he had received a call from a friend who was with Janice, and the friend said he needed to come home. Janice might not make it through the night. Jim called the airlines, and he and the boys left on the first available flight out of Logan.

Jim told me later Janice became conscious before the boys

arrived and explained to her friend how the morning would go. She would need to be propped up with pillows and would bring the boys close for hugs and then they would talk and then she would say it had been a very long morning and they should all take naps. She did not want to let on that she was weak or the end was near. Her friend softly explained the need for a show of strength was over and that she should be fully present in the reality of her story and say good-bye.

Janice sighed and cried and agreed. And when the boys came home, she was sitting up in a chair, but she was not strong for them. She let them be strong for her. And because she had stopped fighting, they were able to be *with* each other.

●　●　●

A week later I was in Florida and checked my e-mail from the hotel room. I received another update from Jim. He was sitting next to his wife, surrounded by the windows that looked out on the forest around his house. Update 53:

> So, I sit in the living room beside her bed, writing and witnessing a beautiful Tennessee morning. It is 15 degrees outside, and the deer are grazing nearby in woods lightly dusted with snow. My precious Janice sleeps, noisily breathing and with difficulty. Her face is drawn, her skin so thin that it is as if all the tiny vessels are ready to break through the surface, her feet and hands cold. She waits. We wait.

During this morning I have been struck with the reality that my wife is not coming back. She will never again sit up and make one of her wisecracks to put me in my place; never laugh with me or respond when asked how long we have been married by saying, "Not long enough." I will never again share her bed, her body; never attend church with her, fly to some faraway city or sit around a dinner table with her and the boys. Regardless of the time left, these things will never again happen. Today I am very sad. Very, very sad.

Still, it is consistent to say, may the peace of Christ bless you and keep you. And today, may you hold those in your house close to your body and feel them breathe and take in their remarkable scent and give them your love.

—JIM

I went to bed that night praying for Jim and for Janice and the boys. The next morning, I checked my e-mail and received Update 54:

This morning at 7:30 a.m. my beautiful, sweet wife, Janice Marie Chaffee, took her last breath and slipped from my arms into the arms of God.

Elliott, Taylor, Bobbie, and our friend Teresa were by her side.

She was quiet, peaceful, and showed no evidence of pain.

Thank you all for your love and prayers; her life has positively and tremendously affected so many.

May the peace of Christ be with us all.

—JIM

Jim and Janice had attended St. Bartholomew Anglican Church outside Nashville for years. I flew in the night before the funeral and the next morning, helped bring in chairs as the pews in the church were filling. I sat with some friends toward the front when Jim and the boys came walking in and took their places. The music was sung from the back, from the balcony, and so seemed to come out of heaven. Jim stood up and read from a poem by W. H. Auden:

> [She] was my North, my South, my East and West
> My working week and my Sunday rest,
> My noon, my midnight, my talk, my song;
> I thought that love would last forever: I was wrong.

•   •   •

That evening a hundred or more of us went back to Jim's home, a large home on a hill surrounded by trees. Elliott, the oldest son, had been thinning the forest since the day his mother died. He'd built an altar of rocks waist-high and kept a fire going out from the kitchen window. When he returned from the funeral, he changed into jeans and started the fire again. Some of us stood on the back deck and watched him pull the starter rope on the chain saw and then cut and drag whole limbs back toward the fire. He would occasionally put down the saw and walk up the stairs to thank somebody for coming. He would stand and look them in the eye and listen to their condolences in such a way it brought them comfort.

Taylor, the younger son, sat in a chair with a glass of wine and talked with his parents' friends about his mom and seemed to enjoy putting the characters in her life together, as though fleshing out lesser-known scenes in her narrative.

Jim and Janice were a part of a food club, a small group of couples who met at their varying houses to cook and eat and drink wine, so the food in the kitchen was rich and celebratory. Some of the women gathered around the television in the living room to watch a documentary A&E had featured about the last year of Janice's life. The cameras followed her on a trip to Boston where she, Jim, and the boys visited an aquarium where they were allowed to lean over a tank and pet seals. Taylor's hair was longer then. The women watching the documentary held hands and leaned into each other, and I felt awkward for standing there too long, so I went back outside.

Jim was sitting around a fire pit on the deck telling a story about how Janice had met his friend Steve, who was also sitting in the circle—the same Steve I was writing the movie with. I sat down and heard how they were all in a choir Jim had directed and how they weren't allowed to move during a performance.

They were supposed to lean in and be very still. Steve smiled and covered his mouth as Jim told how, one night Steve stood in the choir, directly behind Janice, a drop of sweat had gathered on the tip of his nose. Steve had stood perfectly still, leaning in with his hands clasped behind his back, watching cross-eyed as the sweat gathered volume and let go to land on Janice's shoulder.

· · ·

Later, at around two in the morning, when there were only a few dozen people left at their house, I looked across the deck at Steve and Ben sitting and talking to Jim, and as they laughed and drank their wine, I wondered how much it costs to be rich in friends and how many years and stories and scenes it takes to make a rich life happen. *You can't build an end scene as beautiful as this by sitting on a couch,* I thought to myself. And I also knew that while this group had experienced a devastating loss, the ones who remained were richer still because of her passing, as though Janice left an emotional inheritance of stories that would continue to be told, stories that would be passed down to her children.

I looked across the deck at Steve sitting and talking to Jim, and as they laughed and drank their wine, I wondered about the story we were writing and wanted even more to write a better story for myself, something that leaves a beautiful feeling even as the credits roll.

thirty-three

All You Have to Do Is Try

HAVING GROWN UP in Texas, I remember when the small town of Odessa won the state high school football championship. Back then the championship game was held in the Astrodome, and thousands of people would come to watch the next set of boys be crowned Texas football royalty. Nearly twenty years later, after having moved to Portland, I was surprised to hear a movie was coming out about the Odessa team. I hadn't known the story intimately; I only knew that Odessa brought a huge number of fans to Houston for the game, and they were a passionate and loud crowd. Just the fact that they'd made a movie about a football team that won a high school championship twenty years earlier meant there was a story I hadn't heard, so I went to see the movie on opening night.

Friday Night Lights was a great movie, really, a great sports movie about a team that overcame unbelievable conflict, including injuries and abusive parents and undue pressure from the football-crazed community. And, of course, it all came down to the last play in the final seconds, just like any good sports movie. Odessa lined up on the goal line and needed to punch the ball in for the win. They hiked the ball and ran left, but the opposition stood them up on the goal line and knocked them back as time ran out. Odessa lost, and I was confused. I specifically remembered the team winning when I was a kid.

But in the movie version, the credits rolled as the team walked around the field, dazed, some of them with tears in their eyes.

I went home and looked up the story and it turned out Odessa had won the state championship the *following* year. I remembered the story correctly, but the screenwriters didn't write about the year I remembered; they didn't write about the year Odessa won the championship game. They wrote about the year they *almost* won.

I wondered why, of course. I found an article online that said the screenwriters wrote about the year Odessa almost won because that year the team *tried* harder. They said the year the team won the story was great, but the year they lost the story was better, because the team that lost had sacrificed more.

Later, when I started learning about how to resolve a story, and when I began thinking about story as a guide for life, I took a lot of comfort in that principle. It wasn't necessary to win for the story to be great, it was only necessary to sacrifice everything.

thirty-four

To Speak Something
into Nothing

A GOOD STORYTELLER speaks something into nothing. Where there is an absence of story, or perhaps a bad story, a good storyteller walks in and changes reality. He doesn't critique the existing story, or lament about his boredom, like a critic. He just tells something different and invites other people into the new story he is telling.

The last time I visited Bob at his home in San Diego, the entire family was living in the garage. The Goffs have a beautiful home, but it was being remodeled; so they'd spent the past six months sleeping on four beds in the place where they used to park their car. They'd actually made the garage feel homey and comfortable, but it was small and cramped, filled with dressers and small beds covered with quilts, folded towels, and clothes set on the beds for lack of storage. As we walked through the house, looking at the remodel, I asked Maria if she was eager to have her home back. She and Bob looked at each other as though to lament that they would all have to go back to their separate rooms. "The kids will be happier," she said, smiling. "But we like the garage." The garage reminded them of "the old days," Bob said. When the children were very young, and before they had any money, Bob had bought a fifteen-foot-wide piece of land that sloped down to the San Diego Bay. He bought the land because the kids loved the water, and they'd asked their dad if they could have a boat. Bob and Maria couldn't afford a boat and a house, so they bought the land, put a port-a-potty on it, and lived in tents for two years, so they could afford to have a boat. It was one of the happiest times of their lives, Bob said.

We went to breakfast at a place on the water, and I asked more questions, hoping to hear more stories about this crazy family. They told me a few stories, and my favorite, one that seems to symbolize so much in a storyteller's life, had to do with a parade the family threw on their street about ten years earlier, a parade that, apparently, has become a tradition.

Bob and the family were sitting around on New Year's Day when one of the kids mentioned she was bored. Bob agreed and said he thought New Year's Day was probably one of the more boring days of the year. He asked the kids what they could do to make New Year's Day less boring.

The kids started tossing out ideas, things like buying a pony or building a rocket ship, and then one of the children mentioned they could have a parade. Getting himself out of buying a pony, perhaps, Bob lit up and said a parade sounded great.

So Bob, Maria, and the kids sat around the dining room table and dreamed up what their parade might look like. They could wear costumes and hold balloons, and maybe they could invite their friends to watch. The kids started talking about what kind of costumes they could make, the more elaborate, the better. And Maria began planning a cookout at the end of the parade, in their backyard, and wondered how many people she should prepare for. And the kids started running the friends and neighbors they could call to invite them to watch the parade.

Bob thought about it, though, and realized it's more fun to be *in* a parade than to watch one. So he made a rule: nobody would be allowed to watch the parade. But anybody could participate. So he and the kids walked down their small street and knocked on doors, explaining to neighbors that they were having a parade, and anybody who wanted could be in the parade but nobody would be allowed to watch. I laughed as I imagined Bob standing on their neighbor's porch, explaining that if a parade marched by, please look away. Or join. And surprisingly, plenty of his neighbors agreed to take part. They'd march down the street with Bob's kids and join the cookout in the Goffs' backyard. New Year's Day really is the most boring day of the year, after all.

● ● ●

Bob and the family dressed up in their handmade costumes and walked to the end of the street, where they were joined by a few neighbors, and began marching down the street, converting all parade watchers into parade participants. And by the time they got to their backyard, they had a dozen or more people sitting around, enjoying each other's company and eating hamburgers.

But that isn't the best part of the story. The best part is what has taken place over the last ten years. Today, ten years later, the parade attracts hundreds of participants. People who have left the neighborhood fly back just to march in the parade. The residents on Bob's street have taken the idea so far they select a parade queen—sometimes a woman from the local retirement center, sometimes a woman who just needs to have a day in which she is celebrated—and each year the queen gives a speech. There's even an annual Queen's Brunch at the San Diego Yacht Club in which all the former parade queens gather and tell stories about the parade, about the year they reigned as queen. I'm not making this up. The Goff family turned the most boring day of the year into a community favorite that people mark on their calendars and plan their vacations around.

This last year, Bob said to me, smiling, the street's mailman was chosen as the grand marshal and showed up in full uniform, leading the parade by throwing envelopes into the air. After we talked that day, Bob e-mailed me a picture of the parade, and sure enough, the picture revealed hundreds of people marching down his street dressed in costumes under arches of balloons, carrying flags and banners. And as I looked closely at the picture, I noticed there wasn't a single person sitting on the curb. Indeed, nobody was allowed to watch the parade.

I like that part of Scripture that talks about God speaking something into the nothingness, into the dark void. It reminds me of Bob, honestly, walking through the void of New Year's Day.

•   •   •

A good storyteller doesn't just tell a better story, though. He invites other people into the story with him, giving them a better story too.

When we were in Uganda, I went with Bob to break ground on a new school he was building. The school board was there, along with the local officials. The principal of the school had bought three trees that Bob, the government official, and the principal would plant to commemorate the breaking of the ground. Bob saw me standing off, taking pictures of the event and walked over and asked if I would plant his tree for him.

"Are you sure?" I asked.

"Absolutely," he said. "It would be great for me to come back to this place and see the tree you planted, to be reminded of you every time I visit."

I put down my camera and helped dig the hole and set the tree into the ground, covering it to its tiny trunk. And from that moment on, the school was no longer Bob's school; the better story was no longer Bob's story. It was my story too. I'd entered into the story with Bob. And it's a great story about providing an education to children who would otherwise go without. After that I donated funds to Bob's work in Uganda, and I'm even working to provide a scholarship to a child I met in a prison in Kampala who Bob and his lawyers helped free. I'm telling a better story with Bob.

Nobody gets to watch the parade.

thirty-five

Summer Snow in Delaware

ON THE NIGHT before my friends and I rode into Washington, D.C., we were reflective. It didn't feel like we'd ridden across the country. It didn't feel like the ocean was only two days away. We'd grown into the lifestyle and gotten lost in the story and even, to some degree, grieved that it was ending. When you fly across the country in an airplane the country seems vast, but it isn't vast. It's all connected by roads one can ride a bike down. If you watch the news and there's a tragedy at a house in Kansas, that guy's driveway connects with yours, and you'd be surprised how few roads it takes to get there. The trip taught us that we were all neighbors, that my life is connected to everybody else's, that one person's story has the power to affect a million others.

We rode through cities, though Dallas and Little Rock and

Nashville, and we ate at diners and roadside cafés. We rode through Joshua Tree National Park, and I put the U2 album on my iPod, and it made the miles go faster. We had a thousand conversations with people at gas stations, half of them thinking we were lying when we told them where we were going, or once we made it east, where we'd come from. We rode into the sunrise every morning and kept riding until it set into the same ocean we'd left only days before.

We rode our bikes through Kelly's Ford, where two thousand Union troops had crossed the Rappahannock to attack eight hundred Confederates on the march to Gettysburg. We rode along the Rappahannock in the late afternoon with the sun coming in through the pines, and I kept smelling campfire smoke and imagined the battle camps that must have been sewn into the trees along the river.

Every day of the trip was its own epic story. We woke up with an ambition, to move another hundred miles across the map, and we entered into each day's conflict, sometimes getting off the bike to vomit, only to drink more water and get back on the bike. There were positive and negative turns, sunrises in the desert where the color comes up so otherworldly you wonder if you are on another planet, and there were bike accidents that landed friends in the hospital. There were close calls, stolen bikes, and there were always the kind hands of strangers giving us food and water and a place to sleep for the night. And each day's story, each positive and negative turn, was shaping our character. We were becoming people with will and resolve. Our story demanded that we change, and so we did.

Last year, I read a book about a man named Wilson Bentley, who coined the phrase "No two snowflakes are alike." He is the one who discovered the actual reality that no two snowflakes are geometrically the same. Bentley was a New England farmer who fell in love with the beauty and individuality of snow-flakes. In his lifetime, he captured and painstakingly photo-graphed more than five thousand crystals of snow, often submitting his pictures and having them published in various science journals. But his work wasn't purely scientific. He was quite passionate about snowflakes. In one paper—a scientific paper, mind you—he used the words *beauty* or *beautiful* more than forty times.

What amazed Bentley was the realization that each snow-flake bore the scars of its journey. He discovered that each crystal is affected by the temperature of the sky, the altitude of the cloud from which it fell, the trajectory the wind took it as it fell to earth, and a thousand other factors. Bentley would capture his snowflakes on a glass plate and photograph them before they melted, often printing his photos and numbering them, commenting lavishly about their characteristics.

•   •   •

When we arrived in D.C., we rode from the outskirts of town across the Potomac to the Jefferson Memorial. I think we talked less that day than we'd talked on any in seven weeks. There wasn't any complaining, and none of us had our heads down. We rode with our heads toward the monuments, all the altars of our history.

If a story sets our moral compass, my compass had changed from cynicism to hope. I didn't believe the television pundits anymore. I didn't believe people were by nature bad or my neighbor was my enemy. The America we see on television and read about in the newspapers isn't the America we found as we pedaled across the country at fifteen miles per hour. We encountered no fear or tension. Instead, in the small towns stitched together by back roads, we found kindness. By the time we reached Delaware, we'd raised nearly $200,000, most of it coming from small donations, from complete strangers, all to help other strangers who lived an ocean away.

On one afternoon, we'd come off the caprock in Texas and were fighting a headwind, when I met a woman who, even in her simple job behind the counter at a gas station, was telling a better story. I'd been riding for ten hours and was tired and thirsty, and I stopped at this place to get a Coke. She took my money and asked what I was doing riding a bike in the middle of nowhere, and when I told her, she pulled a twenty-dollar bill from her pocket before I could give her a full answer.

"I can't imagine how terrible it would be to live without clean water," she said.

I thanked her and sat down at a bench and table in the

store. I fell asleep with my head on the table. When I woke up, I heard the woman talking to another woman at the counter, and she was explaining her car had been repossessed that morning. As I continued listening to their conversation, I realized the woman had given me her last twenty dollars.

On our last day, after seven weeks of pedaling eight to ten hours each day, we stopped on the side of the road by a Dairy Queen. We knew we only had five miles to go, and none of us believed it was about to end. We circled up with our heads down, none of us knowing what to say. Somebody said we should say a prayer, thanking God for our safety, and we said a prayer. Then we asked Mike Barrow if he would guide us in. We said he had inspired us, and we told him we loved him, and we said we'd be honored if we could follow him for the next five miles, where we'd ride into the Atlantic Ocean. Mike started crying, and so we all started crying. We got back on our bikes and descended on the Delaware shore, weaving in and out of each other's path like falling snow, all of us holding our cameras and throwing our helmets into the shrubs along the roads.

Soon we rode into a state park where we could smell the ocean. We weaved through the parking lot at the back of the park and crashed our bikes into the dunes. We lifted our bikes onto our backs and climbed the hills of sand to see the rocks jetting out into the waves, and a lighthouse a quarter mile off the coast, as though it were there to guide us into the ocean.

Iron Mike looked back and smiled at me. I have never seen a man more happy. His eyes were red and wet, and his face was unshaven, and he was all laughter. Finally, he turned and took us into the water.

---

thirty-six

Where Once
There Was Nothing

I READ A Ray Bradbury book about writing that said writing should be fun. I've never had fun writing a book. I've had fun promoting books, doing readings—that sort of thing—but the truth is I drag myself to the computer. I get up every morning, brush my teeth, and then go back into my bedroom to wake the writer part of me. He's still in bed, snoring, slobbering all over the pillows. I rock him from the shoulders at first, and when that doesn't work, I make some noise, and when that doesn't work, I pull the covers off him and yell proverbs about how poverty comes to the sloth. That usually works, but it's a stretch to call the process fun. I don't know what drugs Ray Bradbury is on, but I'd like to.

I've wondered for a long time why it is that writers hate to write. William Zinsser says that writers "love to have written," and I agree with that.

· · ·

I don't think it's any different when it comes to real-life stories. It would be easier not to try, not to get out of bed. I wish I could tell you I woke every morning and jumped into the thrill a character might feel inside a page-turner, but I don't. I wake every day and plod through the next page of my story, both in words and in actions. I write thank-you cards for The Mentoring Project, I attend board meetings, I take my dog, Lucy, for a walk, I watch television a little. I spend a few hours working on my writing projects. Life doesn't feel meaningless, though. In fact, I like the pace of it. The other day I told Jordan it'd been a year since I'd had a very sad thought. Jordandidn't believe me. He spent the next hour reading me stories on the internet about what happens to kittens when they are picked up by animal control. I honsetly had no idea it was that bad. But it has been a year since I've had a very sad thought. It's probably been a year since my adrenaline pumped too. Bob invited me to ride motorcycles across the Middle East, so maybe my adrenaline will pump if I do that. It sounds like a good next chapter to my story, but I don't know. Who wants to mess with contentment? I might just buy a bottle of wine and listen to a record. I like slower stories these days. I like the simple ones, the ones that play out like art films.

I asked Steve what he wanted people to feel when they finished watching our movie, and he said he wanted people to feel grateful. "Grateful for the film?" I asked. But he said, "No, grateful they are *alive*." That's how I felt on the plane, flying home from the bike trip. I felt grateful. And when we had a banquet for The Mentoring Project in which we thanked our mentors, I felt grateful to be part of such a beautiful story.

•   •   •

Nearly every day in the summer, I take my dog to Westmoreland Park, where she plays in the creek. She runs up and down through the creek bed, diving headlong into the water, chasing ducks. Sometimes when I watch her I think about how good life can be, if we only lose ourselves in our stories. Lucy doesn't read self-help books about how to be a dog; she just *is* a dog. All she wants to do is chase ducks and sticks and do other things that make both her and me happy. It makes me wonder if that was the intention for man, to chase sticks and ducks, to name animals, to create families, and to keep looking back at God to feed off his pleasure at our pleasure.

It's interesting that in the Bible, in the book of Ecclesiastes, the only practical advice given about living a meaningful life is to find a job you like, enjoy your marriage, and obey God. It's as though God is saying, *Write a good story, take somebody with you, and let me help.*

Sometimes, when I'm writing stories, it feels this way. I mean, when I'm sitting at the computer like I am now, I lose track of time and feel as though I'm jumping through the water in the creek, while God is sitting on the shore, pleased at my pleasure.

Before I learned about story, I was becoming a fatalist. I was starting to believe you couldn't feel meaning in life because there wasn't any meaning to be found. But I don't believe that anymore. It's a shame, because you can make good money being a writer and a fatalist. Nietzsche did it with relative success. Not personal success, mind you, because he rarely got out of bed. But he's huge with twenty-something intellectuals. He's the Justin Timberlake of depressed Germans, and there are a lot of depressed Germans.

I don't ever want to go back to believing life is meaningless. I know there are biochemical causes for some forms of depression, but I wish people who struggle against dark thoughts would risk their hopes on living a good story—by that I mean finding a team of people doing hard work for a noble cause, and joining them. I think they'd be surprised at how soon their sad thoughts would dissipate, if for no other reason than they didn't have time to think them anymore. There would be too much work to do, too many scenes to write.

In addressing men in his concentration camp, Victor Frankl,

whom I talked about earlier, spoke of the need to move their thoughts beyond their own despondency, into direct action that affirmed a greater meaning in life:

> We had to learn ourselves and, furthermore, we had to teach the despairing men, that it did not really matter what we expected from life, but rather what life expected from us. We needed to stop asking about the meaning of life, and instead think of ourselves as those who were being questioned by life—daily and hourly. Our answer must exist, not in talk and meditation, but in right action and right conduct. Life ultimately means taking the responsibility to find the right answers to its problems and to fulfill the tasks which it constantly sets before each individual.

We live in a world where bad stories are told, stories that teach us life doesn't mean anything and that humanity has no great purpose. It's a good calling, then, to speak a better story. How brightly a better story shines. How easily the world looks to it in wonder. How grateful we are to hear these stories, and how happy it makes us to repeat them.

Afterword

I DON'T WONDER anymore what I'll tell God when I go to heaven, when we sit in the chairs under the tree, outside the city. I'll tell him about Mike Barrow riding his bike into the Atlantic Ocean, and about Bob Goff and his family jumping off the dock, waving good-bye to world leaders as they left the lodge. I'll ask God if he remembers when I fell apart in the hotel room in Los Angeles, and he'll look comfortingly at me and tell me he was there. I'll tell him about Jason and his family, about breaking ground on the orphanage in Mexico, and about my friends drilling wells in Africa. I'll tell him about The Mentoring Project, how quiet the kids are when they meet their mentors, and how we can't get them to stop talking only a month later. I'll tell these things to God, and he'll laugh, I think, and he'll remind me of the parts I forgot, the parts that were his favorites. We'll sit and remember my story together, and then he'll stand and put his arms around me and say, "Well done," and that he liked my story. And my soul won't be thirsty anymore.

Finally, he'll turn, and we'll walk toward the city, a city he will have spoken into existence, a city built in a place where once there'd been nothing.

About the Author

DONALD MILLER IS the author of *Blue Like Jazz, Searching for God Knows What, Through Painted Deserts,* and *To Own a Dragon.* He is the founder of The Mentoring Project and serves on President Barack Obama's task force on Fatherhood and Healthy Families. He lives and works in Portland, Oregon.

For more information about The Mentoring
Project, or to partner with them to provide
a mentor for a child, please visit
www.thementoringproject.org.

For more information about the movie Don,
Steve, and Ben have written, please visit
www.bluelikejazzthemovie.com.

Acknowledgments

MY CAREER, AND for that matter my life was stalled before I met Steve Taylor and Ben Pearson. I am not sure where I would be if it weren't for their friendship. I certainly wouldn't have written this book. Thank you for helping me write my story, in more ways than one.

I'm grateful as well to the people at Thomas Nelson Publishers, to Brian Hampton and his team who were patient and encouraging through the process of drafting manuscript after manuscript. And to Bryan Norman, for going over each thought and helping me believe this was a story worth telling, and to Kathie Johnson for supporting him so amazingly with countless details throughout the process. Thank you to Michael Hyatt, Heather Adams, Gabe Wicks, and Kristi Henson. And thank you to the sales teams—you do so much to get my books into bookstores and even more to build support with retailers so my message gets a chance. I am truly thankful.

Thank you Tara Brown, Jim Chaffee and Kathryn Helmers, as well as Dan Raines and Eric Goss who keep my life organized and productive. Working wasn't supposed to be this fun.

I'm grateful to the Ride:Well Team. There are more countries to cross and I want to cross them with you. Thank you to Mike Barrow, Criselda Vasquez, Jesse and Brianne Olson, Erin McDermott, Greg Bargo, Brandon Bargo, David Van Buskirk, Margie Gordner, Jen Tyler, Drew Nelson, Jessica Abt, Matthew Williams, Gregg Mwendwa, Jessica Blocker, Joanne Candicamo and Mindy Gunter. Thank you to Jena Lee Nardella at Blood:Water Mission, Gary Haugen at International Justice Mission, Duncan Campbell at Friends for the Children, Jim Bisenius at Common Sense Investments, Aaron Smith at Venture Expeditions, the people at Restore International, Lance Armstrong and The Livestrong Foundation, Catherine Rohr at Prison Entrepeneururship Program, and Josh Shipp at www. joshshipp.com for telling the world stories worth retelling in this book, and for resetting the moral compass for each of us. I also want to thank Tom Ritchey, of Project Rwanda, who is a story all his own, and whose story inspires mine.

I'm grateful for the team of geniuses that make up The Mentoring Project. Thank you to our mentors, to our single moms and our church partners and our staff that is editing the story of fatherlessness in America. Without Dr. John Sowers, Kurt Nelson, Shaun Garman, Justin Zoradi, Wade Trimmer and Hannah Harrod, innumerous children, for many generations, would grow up without positive male role models. The story you are writing will change the world.

Jordan Green, thank you for letting me write about you, and for being such a great character, both in books and in life.

Robert McKee, thank you for taking the time to talk through this book, for agreeing and disagreeing, and for unleashing on the world so many students, who learned from you to tell so many wonderful stories.

I'd like to thank James Scott Bell, as well, for his book *Plot and Structure,* which was a great service to me in learning to write and live better stories.

Thank *you* for continuing to read my books. You have given me the greatest life I could imagine. I love doing this work, and I hope to keep doing it for a long time. Without you, I'd be nowhere. I am so very grateful.

And lastly I want to thank Bob Goff. You are the best storyteller I know. I want you to write a book of your own so people will finally believe the stories I tell about you are true. I love you and your family, and am thankful you've adopted yet another misfit into your tribe. May God continue to bless your story, and may it be retold in the lives of millions.

For a tiny glimpse of what Bob is up to, please visit www.restoreinternational.org

Further Resources

Donald Miller's website:
www.donaldmillerwords.com

Donald Miller's blog:
www.donmilleris.com

Donald Miller on twitter:
@donmilleris

INTO THE ELEMENTS

A 4-part DVD workshop for writers is available in which Donald Miller explains how the elements of story are utilized in both writing and speaking. For more information, please visit: www. intotheelements.com